DEPRESSION AMERICA

DEPRESSION AMERICA

Volume 3

COUNTRYSIDE AND CITY

GROLIER
EDUCATIONAL

About This book

The Great Depression is one of the most important periods of modern U.S. history. Images of breadlines and hungry families are as haunting today as they were at the time. Why did the crisis occur in the world's richest country, and how has it shaped the United States today? *Depression America* answers these questions and reveals a highly complex period in great detail. It describes the uplifting achievements of individuals, tells touching stories of community spirit, and illustrates a rich cultural life stretching from painting to movie-making.

Each of the six volumes covers a particular aspect of the period. The first traces the causes of the Depression through the preceding decades of U.S. history. The second examines the first term of Franklin D. Roosevelt and the New Deal he put in place to temper the effects of the crisis. The third volume studies how the Depression affected the lives of ordinary Americans. Volume 4 reveals the opposition FDR faced from both the political right and left, while Volume 5 explores the effect of the period on U.S. society and culture. The final volume places the Depression in the context of global extremism and the outbreak of World War II, the effects of which restored the United States to economic health.

Each book is split into chapters that explore their themes in depth. References within the text and in a See Also box at the end of each chapter point you to related articles elsewhere in the set, allowing you to further investigate topics of particular interest. There are also many special boxes throughout the set that highlight particular subjects in greater detail. They might provide a biography of an important person, examine the effect of a particular event, or give an eyewitness account of life in the Depression.

If you are not sure where to find a subject, look it up in the set index in each volume. The index covers all six books, so it will help you trace topics throughout the set. A glossary at the end of each book provides a brief explanation of important words and concepts, and a timeline gives a chronological account of key events of the period. The Further Reading list contains numerous books and useful web sites to allow you to do your own research.

Published 2001 by Grolier Educational
Sherman Turnpike
Danbury, Connecticut 06816

© 2001 Brown Partworks Limited

Set ISBN: 0-7172-5502-6
Volume ISBN: 0-7172-5505-0

Library of Congress Cataloging-in-Publication Data
Depression America
     p. cm.
     Includes indexes
     Contents: v. 1. Boom and bust – v. 2. Roosevelt's first term – v. 3. Countryside and city – v. 4. Political tensions – v. 5. U.S. society – v. 6. The war years and economic boom.
     ISBN 0-7172-5502-6 (set : alk. paper)
     1. United States–Economic conditions–1918-1945–Juvenile literature. 3. New Deal, 1933-1939–Juvenile literature. 4. Working class–United States–Juvenile literature. 5. United States–Social life and customs–1918-1945–Juvenile literature. [1. Depressions–1929. 2. New Deal, 1933-1939. 3. United States–History–1919-1933. 4. United States–History– 1933-1945. 5. United States–Economic conditions– 1918-1945.]

HC106.3 D44 2001
330.973'0916–dc21
                                              00-046641

For information address the publisher:
Grolier Educational, Sherman Turnpike, Danbury, Connecticut 06816

Printed and bound in Singapore

For Brown Partworks
Volume consultant: Dr. Victor W. Geraci, Central Connecticut State University
Managing editor: Tim Cooke
Editors: Claire Ellerton, Edward Horton, Christine Hatt, Lee Stacy
Designers: Sarah Williams, Lynne Ross
Picture research:
Becky Cox, Helen Simm, Daniela Marceddu
Indexer: Kay Ollerenshaw

CONTENTS

1

TOUGH IN THE CITY

After the stock-market crash of October 1929 the industry that powered the cities slowed, and the streets filled with the homeless and unemployed. As depression tightened its grip on the nation people looked for support to their personal, family, and friends' resources. Once those were exhausted, America's urban poor had to turn to state and federal government agencies.

The effects of the 1929 stock-market crash brought urban Americans face-to-face with the shortcomings of society's approach to crisis. The outlook of the United States since the early years of the century had been summed up in the notion of individualism: People looked after themselves and their family and relied on their own enterprise, rather than state or federal support, to see them through hard times. At the first signs of the impending economic calamity Americans turned to traditional forms of assistance: their savings; former employers and their "welfare capitalism," whereby they took care of their workers; extended family members; and private charitable organizations. The scale of the economic crisis was beyond the ability of this familiar network of charity to cope with, however. While farmers struggled to make a living (see Chapter 2, "Shadow over the Countryside"), many rural Americans sought work in the cities. There, however, life could be just as tough.

1. COPING WITH CRISIS

Firms of all sizes responded to the October 1929 stock-market crash with mass firings. In November the Willys plant in Toledo, Ohio, reduced its workforce by 85 percent, releasing 24,000 workers. By December Ford Motors had expelled 28,000 workers into the cold winter, cutting its payroll by nearly a quarter. In city after city industries closed their doors to workers, adding almost two million Americans to the unem-

A destitute man leaning against a vacant store, 1935. Closed-down businesses and homeless, unemployed people were a familiar sight on the streets of America's cities during the 1930s.

Customers wait for service at the Dunbar National Bank in Harlem, owned by and for African Americans, January 1933.

ployment lists in the first five months following the crash.

The millions of new unemployed faced the early months of the Depression with resolve. Like President Herbert Hoover, they had little reason to believe that the crisis was anything other than short-term (see Volume 1, Chapter 7, "Hoover: The Search for a Solution"). American history had taught them that hard times built character. They believed that they could count on their own savings, their families, and the arrangements of welfare capitalism to see them through.

Reliance on Savings

Although millions of people had gambled on the stock market in the 1920s, millions more had saved their money wisely. They had deposited billions of dollars in banks and neighborhood associations for rainy-day needs and emergencies.

Such associations offered life insurance policies and collected, invested, and loaned money in their neighborhoods. When the stock market crashed, however, many banks and associations collapsed too.

BANKS FAIL

The 659 banks that failed in 1929 took with them their savers' deposits, which were not protected by any insurance system. Some banks closed with the stock-market crash because they had loaned to failing corporations; some had invested in the stock market themselves; others depended on loans being repaid by workers who were now unemployed; and many had invested in the real-estate market, which plummeted as unemployment skyrocketed. When depositors withdrew more money than the bank held in reserve, the banks closed; and as more banks closed, more investors withdrew

their deposits, creating a downward spiral.

Investors had to withdraw their money in the early years of the Depression. Some had to pay their brokers the 90 percent margin they had borrowed on now-worthless stock. The unemployed withdrew their money for everyday use: to feed themselves, buy warm clothes, make car payments, and pay the rent or mortgage on their homes. After the crash, however, banks did not have enough cash reserves to meet depositors' needs, having loaned out too much before it.

In city after city lines of depositors formed outside banks, surrounding whole blocks, as people tried to get their cash

Banks for Ethnic Communities

Neighborhoods in American cities often contained concentrated ethnic, racial, or economic groups, and banks and associations reflected these community groupings. In Chicago, for example, workers put their money in the First Italian State Bank, the Lithuanian Universal State Bank, the Jewish Noel State Bank, the Czech Novak and Stieskal State Bank, and many others. Building and loan associations also reflected community identities with names like the Lithuanian Dollar Savings Building and Loan Association or the Italo-American Building and Loan Association.

before it disappeared. Often they were too late. A newspaper reported the closure of one of the nation's largest banks serving an African American neighborhood: "Two uniformed policemen were out on guard for several days. There were no disorders. Instead, there was a deathlike pall that hung over those who had entrusted their life savings [to the bank]." With no savings and no jobs, many urban Americans now had to look to their families and local communities.

Financial Survival

As families lost their savings, they prepared for hard times. They still believed in individualism, seeing charity as a sign of failure, and preferred to struggle alone. Thus, after spending whatever money they had, families began to go into debt. Some borrowed from their former employers, others from

family members, and many borrowed money on their life-insurance policies. When recovery did not come and they could borrow no more, they began to liquidate—or exchange for cash—their everyday assets.

The typical unemployed worker began by cashing in any life-insurance policies. Then families gathered their most expensive items and asked the pawn shop to loan them money on any jewels or good clothes they might own. As the Depression continued and food and rent costs became a priority, families forfeited their pawned goods and sold their furniture. They asked stores to give them credit for food, and had to plead with landlords and creditors to postpone evicting them from their homes. If the store was a locally owned shop that a family had frequented in

prosperous times, or the creditor was a fraternal organization that a family member had joined, credit might be granted. If the store was part of a chain or a bank was not local, credit was harder to get and eviction more likely. As the Depression wore on, however, even local shops and associations closed their doors, making self-reliance even more difficult for those struggling through the hard times.

With each passing year more small stores, businesses, and banks closed, causing more families to find self-reliance impossible. As one father wrote to the governor of Pennsylvania in 1931, "I have six little children to take care of. I have been out of work for over a year and a half. Am back almost thirteen months [in rent] and the landlord says if I don't pay up before the 1 of 1932 out I must go, and where am I to go in the cold winter with my children?"

PRIVATE CHARITIES

No longer self-reliant, many Americans nevertheless tried to remain free of government charity by relying on their connections to local religious and ethnic communities. Catholic, Jewish, and other ethnic organizations helped their own. The *Sunday Jewish Courier* proudly informed its readers about its role in helping the millions of impoverished American Jews: "We are good citizens and good Jews, and, therefore, we do not burden the community with our helpless; we maintain charity institutions of

A man sells trousers from a baby carriage on the streets of New York in 1930. Many families, having lost their jobs and life savings following the stock-market crash, were forced to sell their possessions to pay the rent and buy food.

Evictions

Evictions became commonplace. By 1932 banks foreclosed on nearly 750 homes every day. In early 1933 the figure had increased to 1,000 a day as the national percentage of city dwellers who defaulted on their home loans climbed toward 20 percent: 60 percent of Alabamans living in Birmingham defaulted on their home loans, and 62 percent of Cleveland's homeowners stopped paying their mortgages.

Tenants were evicted from rented houses and apartments in every city. Who could afford to pay rent? A report in the *New York Times* (February 2, 1932) captured the drama of evictions, reporting the use of 50 detectives and patrolmen to help ten movers do their job: "Women shrieked from the windows, the different sections of the crowd hissed and booed and shouted invectives. Fighting began simultaneously in the house and in the street. The Marshall's men were rushed on the stairs and only got to work after the policemen had driven the tenants back into their apartments."

Unemployed families with no income, no savings, and finally no home reluctantly moved into relatives' homes: Aged parents moved into their children's homes; young parents sent their children to live with slightly more prosperous cousins; and several families often joined together and crowded into homes designed for just one. As these overcrowded families struggled, poverty forced the occupants to turn for assistance to neighbors and neighborhood associations.

our own." Rabbis and pastors asked their congregations to compile lists of jobs that members might have open at a store or around the home, while prosperous members of congregations organized social dinners to feed their poorer members. Barbers might provide a free haircut on occasion to a member of the congregation, or the baker might send day-old bread to a needy family, the butcher might have some odds and ends of meat, and the tailor might have some spare clothing. Again, however, as each year of the early thirties brought greater poverty, charity organizations had to turn to city and state governments for funding so that they could continue to help their communities.

WELFARE CAPITALISM

Welfare capitalists, who believed that charity should be controlled by benevolent industrialists and kept out of the hands of the government, belonged to a U.S. tradition of mutualism in which

In May 1933 New York "mortgage marchers" petitioned President Roosevelt for postponement of foreclosures. Despite their action, two-fifths of homeowners in 20 cities had lost their homes by 1934.

people were responsible for supporting their own community. At first companies took responsibility for their own. In Chicago,

Movie star Edward G. Robinson selling dolls for charity, c. 1935. Private charities did what they could to help the poor unemployed by providing free food and clothes, and organizing charity events to raise funds for the needy.

for example, the Armour and Swift meat company sent coal and food to former employees; Oscar Mayer personally handed out sausage links to his hungry former employees; with production reduced, U.S. Steel provided emergency provisions for all its nonworking "employees" who refused to apply to charities; International Harvester set up gardens for its former employees to grow food and offered interest-free loans to those willing to commit to repaying them. Such services came at a price: The same companies reduced benefits such as insurance, reduced the length of the working day, shrank the workforce, and forced their remaining workers to contribute financially to company charity

work. Inevitably, as time dragged on, companies began to reduce the amount of charitable support they provided.

Welfare capitalists appeared at first to be successful not only in helping former employees, but also in helping their local communities by cooperating with private charities. They raised substantial amounts of money to donate to community organizations. Looking to apply local aid to local problems without government help, private charities in New York City raised over $8 million in the Depression's first year; in 1931 city employees and teachers alone contributed almost $2.5 million to private charities. Citizens in Boston raised almost $5.5 million in the first two years of the economic calamity, just a little more than the people of Chicago raised. It was in Phila-

The menu of the first ever Penny Restaurant in New York, pictured in 1931. These restaurants provided cheap food for the poor in the Depression.

delphia, Pa., however, that welfare capitalism seemed to fulfill its pledge the best.

Philadelphia's Committee for Unemployment Relief

Philadelphia, like most major cities, provided its inhabitants with privately sponsored welfare in the early Depression. This was hard to do in the first months because the city's economy had been in a downturn throughout 1929, and unemployment needs had already peaked before the crash. Indeed, emphasizing the fact that the stock-market crash had not itself caused hard times, the city's unemployment level had risen above 10 percent six months before it happened. The city's premier charity, the Philadelphia Family Society, could do no more after the crash than it had before: help 750 new families each month, every month. This situation changed in 1930, when Philadelphia's welfare capitalists became involved in relief.

In November 1930, 200 of Philadelphia's wealthiest industrialists and citizens organized a

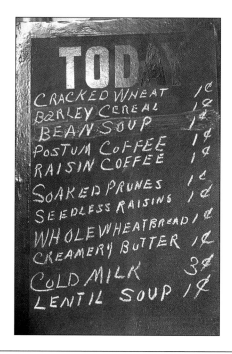

new private charity, which leaders pledged would approach the Depression in the City of Brotherly Love with "the same spirit of fighting as that which engaged Philadelphia during the World

•

"...the same spirit... which engaged Philadelphia during the World War."

•

Regular customers take advantage of a free shave during a barber's strike in New York, c.1930.

War." They created the Committee for Unemployment Relief to combat poverty with charity money from the United Campaign Fund and from those citizens who remained prosperous.

The committee addressed the problems of poverty in an approach outlined by billionaire philanthropist Andrew Carnegie (1835–1918) in his book *The Gospel of Wealth*. Carnegie proposed that relief should extend ladders of self-help, allowing the poor to climb out of poverty by their own actions. The committee created a subcommittee to provide citizens with repayable loans and temporary work, and others to provide direct relief to families, care for homeless individuals, and free breakfasts for poor children.

In its first year the committee spent $3 million. It was not enough to keep pace with growing unemployment: By the end of the year 2,000 new families applied for assistance every week. In its second year the committee spent $5 million in its first three months; it ran out of money and suspended operations. The committee then turned to the local and state gov-

ernments for assistance, acknowledging that welfare capitalism alone could not cope with the financial crisis.

HELP FROM CITY AND STATE

As the Depression wore on, cities began to reconsider their reluctance to rely on nonlocal help. They looked to their state governments for help; later they would look to the federal government. New Orleans' charitable organization, the Welfare Committee, originally accepted only private funds, most of which came from city employees. However, unable to help everyone, it turned to the city government, which raised money by issuing bonds. This local assistance helped but soon evaporated. The committee then turned to the state of Louisiana. By 1932, when state funds were exhausted and the federal government had created a source of funds in the shape of the Reconstruction Finance Corporation (RFC), the committee asked for aid from there too. Similarly, in San Francisco community leaders soon spent the millions of dollars

collected from private charities, notably the Community Chest and the Jewish Fund. Next they turned to the city for money and asked the state of California for over $1 million to fund public works that would provide workers with construction jobs. The city, too, budgeted over $1 million for public works for 1931 and 1932.

The Civic Emergency Committee in Portland, Oregon, was formed to provide private relief but relied on help from local government. Working with the Portland Chamber of Commerce, which provided $25-a-month short-term loans to married heads of families, the committee hired the unemployed to work six eight-hour days a month on public projects in return for $24. As in other cities, when funds ran out, local relief depended on the city and the state to assist the growing numbers of permanently unemployed. As the winter of 1932 to 1933 approached, however, even state governments ran out of funds, and

the cities of the nation increasingly turned to the federal government for help.

2. THE CONTINUING ECONOMIC CRISIS

For three years in a row after the Wall Street Crash the American economy worsened. In 1930 a further 1,352 banks failed; the following year 2,294 more collapsed. Billions of dollars were lost. As the winter of 1932 turned into the spring of 1933, the total number of bank failures exceeded 6,000: About one of every four banks in the nation had closed its doors. In the residential section of Chicago, outside the downtown business "Loop," 163 of the 199 banks had closed by March 1933. With no banks to give them loans, and with no way to raise cash by selling near-worthless stock, tens of thousands of companies that no longer had a domestic market to buy their goods folded.

COMPANIES CUT HOURS AND PAY

In city after city companies desperately looking for ways to stay solvent began to hire only part-time labor. By 1932 the steel industry employed only part-time workers, and only enough of them to produce just 12 percent of the steel being produced before the crash. To protect their profits with such low demand, steel plants not only cut back workers' hours but reduced hourly wages by almost two-thirds. Similar situations faced workers in the auto industry, who had enjoyed nearly full-time employment at about $5 a day before the crash. Ford reduced its workforce by over 70 percent by June 1931; and in December 1932 the Briggs auto plant was paying men 10 cents an hour; women earned only 4 cents an hour.

General contractors before the Depression had earned several

Hundreds of unemployed men wait in line to register at the emergency Unemployment Relief offices in New York, where the police had earlier quelled a riot, on October 2, 1931.

dollars a day, but now brickmakers made 6 cents an hour and millers 5 cents an hour after three desperate years of watching wages diminish.

MORE WOMEN WORKERS

As companies reacted to the Great Depression by reducing wages and numbers of full-time employees, they affected the social composition of the urban work-force. Women had always worked in urban America, and during the Depression more needed to do so. Single women could rely less on emergency help from family members who were themselves destitute. Similarly, the financial contributions of mothers, wives, and children to the family income

Unemployment Figures Rise

Accompanying the closing of banks and industries came the rise of both unemployment and underemployment figures. On average, companies fired 20,000 workers every day of the workweek, every week, for the three years following the crash. The unemployment figures for cities across America rose until, in the winter of 1932, over one million workers were jobless in New York City, representing one-third of the city's workers. In Cleveland, Akron, and Toledo, Ohio, unemployment in 1932 reached 50 percent, 60 percent, and 80 percent respectively. In the same season in Donora, Pennsylvania, the 13,900 precrash workforce fell to a mere 277. Official statistics put the nation's unemployment in 1932 at just over 24 percent; however, even the conservative business-oriented magazine *Fortune* believed the true figure to be well over one-third of the population.

since male managers figured their harassment would not be challenged or reported by women who were desperate to hang on to their jobs. A number of select industries also targeted women as "first cuts" when shedding jobs, believing it more important to retain men. The government endorsed such biased behavior with section 213 of the 1932 Federal Economy Act. This section barred married couples from working for U.S. federal agencies. Three-quarters of those fired as a result were women, some of whom had been earning more than their husbands.

became increasingly vital. Single women often found they had to rent apartments with other single women and sleep in shifts in order to remain self-reliant.

Women found it especially important to be able to rely on themselves because most relief agencies believed that men should be the primary breadwinners and focused their charity efforts mainly on helping males. Nevertheless, because companies traditionally paid women less than men, women sometimes found they had more opportunities to find work because bosses saw them as cheap labor. The number of married women wage-earners actually increased over the course of the Depression by 15 percent.

Sexual Discrimination

Work was far from easy for women during the Depression, however. Most noticed that sexual harassment at work increased,

New York breadline, 1932. In the absence of government relief free food was distributed to the poor with private funds in some cities.

RACIAL DISCRIMINATION

Racial tension flared in America's cities. Embracing the notion of seniority, managers often practiced a "last hired, first fired" policy. This affected recent migrants from rural areas to urban-industrial centers, especially African Americans, who found themselves receiving pink slips— the notices of termination—along with recent immigrants from Asia, Europe, and Mexico. Some, though by no means all, of the layoffs owed more to racism and ignorance than to fairness. Even people who drew up and maintained welfare lists sometimes excluded non-Anglo families from the relief rolls (see Volume 5, Chapter 2, "Equality for Some").

PSYCHOLOGICAL EFFECTS OF THE DEPRESSION

As poverty-stricken Americans turned to charity as a last resort, they experienced enormous psychological depression. Turning to charity was considered the very lowest rung of the social ladder, and those who suffered the most blamed themselves for failing (see Volume 4, Chapter 5, "Welfare").

To maintain their pride, unemployed men and women were known to try to dupe their families by continuing to get ready for work each morning; shortly after leaving home, they would change out of their good clothes and go to the city dump to scavenge for food, look for jobs at agencies, or sell apples on street corners to raise a little change.

There were some people for whom the shame of poverty was too much. Suicide rates had remained fairly constant during the Roaring Twenties, but they rose by 25 percent each year from 1930 to 1932. So many people jumped off the Hanrahan Bridge in Memphis that city newspapers published on their front pages the names of counselors willing to help the suicidal. Another common emotional response to unemployment was desertion of one's family and home. Most of those who left their families were men, but large numbers of women and children also ran away. Many joined the ranks of the urban homeless.

THE HOMELESS

Life on the streets was difficult, and the people who wandered the cities sometimes broke the law deliberately in order to be arrested and cared for. On October 7, 1932, the *New York Times* reported that a group of homeless men sleeping in the city's subway system had been pleased to be arrested: "Fifty four men were arrested yesterday morning for sleeping or idling in the arcade connecting with the subway through 45 West Forty-second

Woolworth employees seem to be enjoying their sit-down strike to win a 40-hour week in 1935. People with jobs faced a constant struggle to preserve their work conditions.

An African American family outside their home in a poor section of Washington, D.C., c.1937. In America in the thirties racial minorities were discriminated against in the areas of employment—getting or keeping a job—and claiming relief.

Street, but most of them considered their meeting with a raiding party of ten policemen as a stroke of luck." Fifteen days earlier the paper had reported that "Policemen, with apologies and good feelings on both sides, arrested for vagrancy 25" homeless people.

HOBO TRAVELERS

When women, men, and children tired of roaming the streets of their native city, or living in garbage dumps, they hit the rails to try their luck at finding a job in another city (see Volume 2, Chapter 4, "Where Did the Depression Bite?").

Millions of children prematurely declared independence from their families and spent the Depression living in ways similar to homeless adults. Hundreds of thousands took to the rails. Mostly men rode the trains, but up to 25 percent of the homeless stealing space on boxcars were children, mainly boys. In 1929 the Mississippi & Pacific railroad company counted 13,745 hobos riding their boxcars. As the Depression got worse, the numbers increased. In 1932 the Southern Pacific ejected 700,000 hobos from their cars.

Arriving in the Cities

As the railroads deposited their illegal riders in central cities, the police rounded up as many as possible. Children faced prosecution like their adult counterparts, although most jumped from the trains as they slowed into stations to avoid being caught. Some police took pity on the child hobos. When Miami officers caught children they took them to the beach for a cleansing swim and then deposited them at the city limits with the warning that if they returned, they would be arrested. Miami threw out an average of at least eight children a day in 1932, but other cities saw much more activity: 3,000 children arrived in Des Moines every year, Los Angeles received 3,000 a month, 5,000 entered New Orleans every month, and 700 poured into Kansas City every day.

Mexican-Americans

Although all ethnic minorities in many cities during the Depression were affected by ethnocentrism, urban Mexican-Americans faced added hardships. Tens of thousands of Mexican-Americans worked in urban-industrial jobs, especially in Los Angeles, Chicago, Detroit, and throughout urban Indiana. Although they exhibited the same pride as other immigrants concerning welfare and avoided it successfully by relying on family connections, city officials across America believed they comprised a significant percentage of those on relief. In reality, in Los Angeles they represented 10 percent of the total population, but only 1 percent of those requesting relief. Nevertheless, urban America rounded up hundreds of thousands of Americans whose ancestors had descended from Mexico and deported them to Mexico, regardless of whether they had immigrated from that country.

An unemployed man lying beside the New York City docks in 1935. Although the whole country was in the grip of a chronic economic depression, Americans felt there was a real stigma attached to being unemployed. Men, in particular, found it hard not to blame themselves for being out of work.

CHILDREN IN THE CITY

The children who stayed home in the city did not always fare much better than their rail-riding peers, particularly if their parents were unemployed or underemployed. Many children had to scavenge for food alongside their parents. Explained an eighth-grade schoolboy from Nashville: "For a whole week one time we didn't have nothing to eat but potatoes. Another time...we ate that dog meat with the potatoes. I went to school hungry and came home to a house where there wasn't any fire." Although many parents went hungry themselves so that they could feed their children, up to 85 percent, and sometimes 90 percent, of schoolchildren were deemed to be underweight.

Poor School Services

City children also suffered from deteriorating educational services. As cities lost revenues normally paid in taxes by thriving companies, the Great Depression crippled education. From 1929 to 1933 school districts slashed the already low salaries of teachers. To save even more money, city officials and school boards crammed 50 or more children into classrooms designed for 30 students. They shortened the school year, and as the winter of 1932 to 1933 set in, they closed schools altogether to save heating bills and fired tens of thousands of teachers. By the end of the winter nearly 3,000 schools had closed; more than 10 million children were denied an educational opportunity.

•

"I went to school hungry...came home to a house where there wasn't any fire."

•

3. GOVERNMENT REACTION

Starving citizens came to despise President Herbert Hoover, whose reputation permanently suffered. In the eyes of his critics Hoover

Charity Soup Kitchens and Lodges

For those who wandered the city streets charities provided soup kitchens and hostels. Mostly men, but women and children too, lined up for hours to receive coffee, a bowl of soup, and some bread.

In Detroit the Fisher Body Company allowed an unused factory to be turned into the Fisher Lodge for several thousand homeless. New York City homeless could turn to the city's Municipal Lodging House, where 128 men were seated in unison and given 25 minutes to consume coffee, soup, and graham crackers. Every 25 minutes, from 4:00 P.M. till late at night, a group of 128 hobos was admitted. After eating, patrons who chose to spend the night forfeited their clothes to be fumigated by the laundry service, took a shower, donned a clean nightshirt, and slept in a common room until breakfast.

Such forms of welfare helped, but were unpleasant: As patrons waited for hours in lines with over a thousand other homeless, hoping to be seated in the little kitchen, the

Fired workers enjoy free food in gangster Al Capone's soup kitchen for the unemployed at 935 State Street, Chicago, November 1930.

bitter cold tore at skin barely covered by inadequate jackets; the disinfectants used to fumigate the clothes stank; and the food, although nourishing, held little appeal. Because welfare lodging was not guaranteed, many people had to find other accommodations, such as park benches and doorways.

The average age of the men in this homeless men's facility in Sioux City, Iowa, was 52. Most were from urban areas. Unemployment was the main reason they were there. Most would have been happy to work if they could find a job.

Hoovervilles

Unemployed and homeless, citizens of Philadelphia sleep in a corridor in City Hall to escape the cold winter of 1931.

During the early years of the depression police often allowed the homeless to shelter in unofficially designated areas, such as parks, alleys, and abandoned buildings. Towns developed made of tarpaper, tin, packing crates, and even old car bodies. Some were squalid and filthy, but families who held out hope for better times ensured their homes were clean and tidy.

In Phoenix the homeless camped under bridges on the Salt River. In Cincinnati they slept in sewer pipes stored above ground. Many destitute families built homes at their local dump. As the homeless took over parks and empty spaces, residents associated their poverty with Herbert Hoover and named their makeshift villages "Hoovervilles."

Seattle Hooverville, Washington, August 1933. The unemployed residents of Seattle constructed this Hooverville just south of downtown and appointed their own mayor and city council to govern it.

The magazine *Forum and Century* noted in its September 1932 issue the following national phenomenon: "...the largest Hooverville in the United States is in St. Louis, with a hovel population of 1,200." Journalist Charles Walker went on to describe the depths of poverty endured by the inhabitants of another Hooverville in Youngstown, Ohio, located at the city dump: "I went forward and talked to the men; they showed me their houses. These vary greatly from mere caves covered with a piece of tin to weather-proof shanties built of packing boxes and equipped with a stolen window-frame or an improved door.... The location of the town also has its commissary advantage; men take part of their food from the garbage house. This I entered; the stench of decaying food is appalling. Here I found that there were more women than men—gathering food for their [traditional] homes [outside the Hooverville]."

By 1932 Americans' contempt for their president showed in the way they began applying the term "Hoover" to their everyday lives. If they slept on a park bench and covered themselves with a newspaper for warmth, they called it a "Hoover blanket." They named their broken-down cars, which they now needed to haul with mules or horses, "Hoover hogs." And when they made "rabbit ears" by pulling the insides of their pant pockets out to reveal they had no money, they said they were flying their "Hoover flags."

carried on as if nothing was wrong. He called on citizens to rely on the spirit of individualism and welfare capitalism, and not turn to the government for aid. The Hoover administration, like many politicians and economists, believed that the Depression was a severe manifestation of the kind of economic downturn that the United States had suffered before. It was part of the economic cycle, as was the recovery that would inevitably follow.

When Secretary of the Treasury Andrew Mellon learned of the stock-market crash of October 1929, he remarked on its positive effects: "People will work harder... and enterprising people will pick up the wrecks from less competent people." Hoover shared the same belief: "Some individuals may have lost their nerve and faith," he commented almost two years after the crash, "but the real American people are digging themselves out with industry and courage."

Hoover originally placed his faith in the mechanisms of welfare capitalism. He commented:

•

"Nobody is actually starving. The hobos... are better fed than they have ever been."

•

"Nobody is actually starving. The hobos, for example, are better fed than they have ever been. One hobo in New York got ten meals in one day!" The president asked the surgeon general, Hugh S. Cumming, to compare the "state of the public health" during the Great

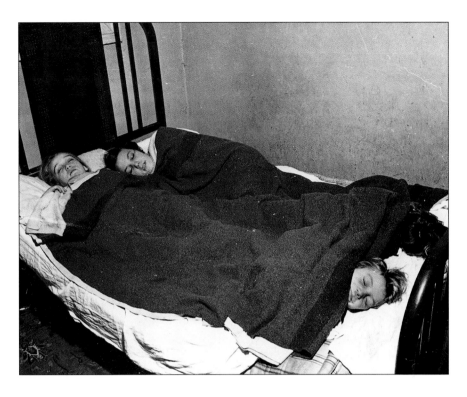

Four members of a family of eleven share a bed in one of 300,000 windowless rooms in New York City's slums. Overcrowded slums were a serious social problem in the United States in the thirties.

Depression to a period in 1928 of full employment. From the incomplete draft of the report Hoover concluded : "The public health has apparently never been better than it has been over the past six months.... It is a most creditable showing of the effort which the country made last winter and one for which the voluntary organizations are entitled to a very great deal of credit." However, he ignored the growing trend in nearly every city: With every passing year companies reduced their welfare services, and charities spent their funds faster than they could raise them.

HOOVER REFUSES FEDERAL AID

Hoover's faith in charity chimed with a traditional belief in limiting the role of government in the nation's life. He wrote, "It is not the function of the government to relieve individuals of their responsibilities to their neighbors, or to relieve private institutions of their responsibilities to the

public." Echoing the words of President Grover Cleveland in 1887, he went on: "The lesson should be constantly enforced that though the people support the Government, the Government should not support the people. The friendliness and charity of our countrymen can always be relied upon to relieve their fellow citizens in misfortune."

There were federal efforts to improve the situation, but Hoover directed them at sustaining morale. "Victory over this depression," he proclaimed on radio, "will be won by the resolution of our people to fight their own battles in their own communities, by stimulating their ingenuity to solve their own problems, by taking new courage to be masters of their own destiny in the struggle of life."

NONFEDERAL AID DRIES UP

Hoover's faith in charity and welfare capitalism became unrealistic as the Depression went on. Companies reduced aid to their employees, and charities ran out of money. In New Orleans charities turned away 2,000 families when they stopped accepting new applicants for assistance. Omaha announced plans to eliminate two-thirds of the names from its relief lists. In Philadelphia the committee received state assistance to re-launch its attack on poverty, but the need for relief outstripped even those funds, leaving 250,000 Philadelphians, including 150,000 children, facing desperate hunger.

In city after city relief agencies cut families off their welfare lists. In Detroit, reported the September issue of *Fortune* magazine, the list of people being dropped from aid "carries or has carried 45 ministers, 30 bank tellers, lawyers, dentists, musicians, and two families after whom streets are named."

FDR'S ELECTION

When Franklin D. Roosevelt won the 1932 election, he was supported by the overwhelming majority of urban Americans. As governor of New York during the first year of the Depression, he had sent the state's money to help provide relief in the cities. He promised a similar national approach now. "No one wants government to assume more functions, but it is clear that government in this nation cannot let its people starve. Government in the United States must not allow its men, women, and children to suffer excessive privation."

The legislation of Roosevelt's famous Hundred Days included numerous measures designed to help urban and rural Americans alike. He staved off a banking crisis; the Home Owners' Loan Corporation temporarily forbade banks from foreclosing on homes and established federal guidelines to help Americans buy and keep their homes; over $15 billion was loaned to businesses on more generous grounds than by Hoover's Reconstruction Finance Corporation; the Roosevelt administration gifted monies to charitable organizations trying to help. Beginning with $500 million, the Federal Emergency Relief Administration eventually donated $5 billion in direct aid to starving Americans. Other job-creation plans were administered by the Civilian Works Administration

Fiorello La Guardia

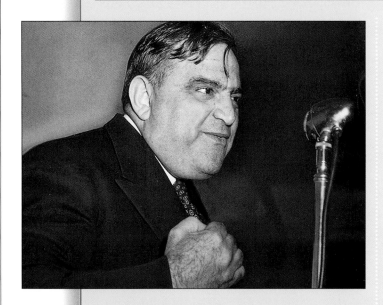

La Guardia earned the affectionate nickname "The Little Flower" on account of his height— he stood just 5 feet 2 inches (1.6m) tall.

Born in New York City and educated at New York University, Fiorello Henry La Guardia (1882–1947) was the son of a U.S. Army bandmaster. Following a spell in Europe, he returned to the United States and in 1916 was elected to the U.S. House of Representatives as a progressive Republican.

After serving with the U.S. Air Service in World War I, La Guardia returned to Congress, where he opposed Prohibition and campaigned for woman suffrage and an end to child labor. In 1932 he joined forces with Senator George Norris in the Norris-La Guardia Act, which curbed the power of the courts to ban strikes.

La Guardia was elected mayor of New York City in 1933, 1937, and 1941. A dedicated social activist, he would often appeal directly to the people of New York on political issues. He retired from the mayoralty in 1945.

(CWA), which in 1933 to 1934 hired four million Americans to improve parks, build public buildings, playgrounds, and swimming pools, and participate in other projects that helped local communities. The Public Works Administration (PWA) put millions to work by contracting work to private companies. The Civilian Conservation Corps (CCC) employed nearly 500,000 young men to work in forest and national parks (see Volume 2, Chapter 5, "Putting People to Work").

CONDITIONS IMPROVE

Roosevelt's programs countered some of the worst deprivations of the Depression. The New Deal, however, suffered accusations that it concentrated too much on agriculture and the problems of rural America, rather than the cities. People still rode the rails and wandered the streets, but there were fewer of them. It would not be until the outbreak of World War II in Europe in 1939 that full employment returned.

4. CHICAGO: A CASE HISTORY

The effects of the Depression and the various sources of relief provision are well illustrated by tracing the decade in a single U.S. city, Chicago. At the time of the Wall Street Crash Chicago had been the nation's leading manufacturing city. The Depression hit jobs badly—by the worst year, 1932, some 750,000 citizens were out of work, compared with only 800,000 who had

Almost 600,000 families were living in 50,000 old-law, overcrowded, dilapidated tenements in New York in 1939. New housing projects would provide for only 8,000 families.

jobs. Only 51 of the city's 228 banks remained open. Private and local relief supported more than 160,000 families. Thousands of

•

"…it is clear that government in this nation cannot let its people starve."

•

people slept in the city parks and scavenged the garbage dumps for food. One witness watched a

crowd of men, women, and children swarming over a garbage truck as it dropped rubbish: "As soon as the truck pulled away from the pile, all of them started digging with sticks, grabbing for garbage and bits of food." Another woman described the odd atmosphere in the city that winter: "I do not know how it may have been in other places…but in Chicago the city seemed to have died. There was something awful—abnormal—in the very stillness of the streets."

The city's African American population, already the victims of years of neglect and poverty, suffered particular hardship. Violence spilled out in August

1931 as leaders of communist-dominated unemployment councils addressed a crowd in Washington Park. The speakers protested against the eviction of an elderly lady for nonpayment of rent. As the meeting went on, the crowd learned that the bailiffs were already moving the woman out of her apartment. A crowd of around 2,000 went to the flat, stopped the eviction, and began returning the woman's furniture. When the police arrived to disperse them, three young black men died. More than 25,000 black mourners attended their funeral. The city administration declared a moratorium on future evictions.

CITY POLITICS

To make matters worse, the city was virtually bankrupt by the end of 1930, partly as a result of supporting the unemployed. Teachers and other city employees worked without pay. The Illinois state government, dominated by rural interests, voted against a state income tax to fund relief. They sold land to raise $20 million, but with unemployment rising to 42 percent the money was gone in three months.

This was the background of the 1931 mayoral election. Against the Republican incumbent, "Big Bill" Thompson, the Democrats ran former street vendor Anton "Tony" Cermak, longtime leader of the city's Czechs and secretary of the antiprohibitionist United Society for Local Self-Government. The nomination split the party. Many of the Democrats' traditional Irish supporters refused to vote for Cermak.

In the campaign both candidates concentrated on trading insults based largely on ethnicity. Referring to the World's Fair scheduled for the state in 1933,

A destitute man scavenging for food on the city dump in Dubuque, Iowa, 1940. Although improvements had been made by the end of the decade, poverty, unemployment, and homelessness were still very much in evidence.

Thompson yelled at Cermak, "Tony, Tony, where's your push-cart at? Can you imagine a World's Fair mayor with a name like that?" Both candidates had links with Chicago's criminal underworld, but reformers favored Cermak. In the words of one Methodist minister, "Cermak is bad but Thompson is worse."

A number of scandals turned voters away from Thompson, but probably what hurt him most was that the Republican Party had been in power when the Depression broke out. Cermak won by the greatest majority in the city's history—671,189 to 476,922.

When Cermak took over the city, his priority was to balance the budget. He fired over 2,000 "temporary employees" appointed by his predecessor, but soon the demands of patronage forced him to replace them with a similar number of his own. He cut most city employees' salaries by 20 percent and eliminated sick leave and vacations.

When FDR was elected in 1932, Cermak met the president and observed, "Roosevelt is not only weak in the legs, he's also weak in the head." The next time the pair met, an assassin fired a gun at Roosevelt but hit Cermak, who died 19 days later, on March

Selling on the Street

Gipsy Lineberry was born in the Blue Ridge Mountains of Virginia but in 1932 moved to Washington, D.C., to find work: "Well, I came here looking for a job, and this fella hired about six of us to go out and sell radios…. I'd go over to Third Avenue, and I'd have people stop me and say, 'Hey, you the radio man? How about one of them radios?' I said, 'Well, you got any money?' 'Oh, I got $15.' 'Well, give me the $15 and next week when you get enough for the $35, I'll give you the radio.' It was a [GE] battery set…. They played them night and day, and eventually the battery went dead, and they wouldn't make the payment. So that's when I quit and went into hotel work."

6, 1933. The Democrats in Chicago then elected as mayor Edward J. Kelly, an Irish politician with a history of patronage and graft.

FEDERAL FUNDS

The city's relief funds were exhausted; but late in 1933, as part of FDR's New Deal, Congress created the Federal Emergency Relief Administration (FERA) to distribute relief funds to local communities. States had an obligation to provide a minimum of matching funds, however, and Illinois's rural interests were reluctant to impose the new taxes necessary to do so. When FERA threatened to suspend all federal relief payments, the state lawmakers passed a bond issue rather than raising tax.

Harold Ickes, head of FERA, was reluctant to give federal funds directly to city governors. He believed that local politicians were often corrupt and would use the money to increase their own power. Harry Hopkins' Civil Works Administration was more willing to spend money to alleviate suffering in the winter of 1933 to 1934. Some 76,000 people in Chicago worked for the agency, mainly on street repair and snow-shoveling. In 1935 the Works Program Administration took over the role of providing public works relief.

BUILDING A PARTY MACHINE

True to Ickes's fears, Democratic politicians in Chicago used the influx of federal capital for themselves. Kelly and his advisor Pat Nash built a political machine. In 1936 *Fortune* magazine described it as "an organization that trades philanthropy (with other people's money) for votes." Politicians provided jobs and relief in return for support, hiring workers on largely political grounds.

The success of the Kelly-Nash organization became apparent in the election of 1936. Kelly promised no new taxes, arguing that the city could get all the money it needed from the federal government and blame national politicians for any tax rises necessary to fund it. The Republicans were barely able to find a

•

"Hey, you the radio man? How about one of them radios?"

•

candidate to run against him. Kelly received the support of every major newspaper and every ethnic group. He carried every ward in the city and won 75.3% to 17.2%; the city council had only five Republican members.

Kelly's ability to deliver votes made him popular with Democrats in Washington who were expecting a close presidential election in 1936 (see Volume 2, Chapter 6, "The Election of 1936"). They sent more funds to the city. Meanwhile the state legislature steadfastly refused to increase taxes. Relief offices in the city closed as state and local officials argued over how much each should pay.

A NEW RECESSION

In 1937 cutbacks in federal spending led to a new recession and increasing unemployment. In Chicago relief payments had to be cut to meet all the applications; the amount given to each recipient was only 85 percent of the amount required to support a minimum standard of living. In

1938, 200,000 families were on relief. Almost one in every six Chicagoans received some form of public aid. The renewed recession again pushed the city to the verge of bankruptcy. It was only when the approach of war in Europe began to raise demand in 1939 that industry began to recover.

DEFENDING THE NEW DEAL

Chicago's Republicans decided to fight the 1939 mayoral election by attacking the effect of FDR's policies on the city. Their candidate was Dwight Green, a one-time federal district attorney who in the 1920s had led the case that sent mobster Al Capone to Alcatraz (see Volume 3, Chapter 5, "Crime in the Depression"). Green presented himself as the

Maxwell Street market, in a poor part of Chicago, around 1930, when unemployment had made poverty a serious problem in the city.

Selling Clothes to Eat

Gipsy Lineberry moved to a hotel as a cashier. "A lot of people who lived there were retirees.... Oh, lots of times I would loan them a dollar to go over to Sholl's, the cafeteria, to buy lunch. They were so broke.... I remember one fella had been a manager of a clothing store. [His] store had gone out of business. He came down one day with a full tuxedo, with suspenders, shirt studs, everything. He threw it across the desk, and he said, 'Would you give me $5 for that?' I put it on. It fit perfect. Brand new. It didn't look like it had ever been worn. I gave him $5 for it."

spokesperson of the people against the Democrat machine, its bosses, and its funders. The Democrats, for their part, ran a low-key campaign that focused on the national situation. "Show that Chicago is behind President Roosevelt," urged Kelly's campaign slogan. He was also careful to stress that a Democrat government would maintain the flow of federal funds to the city, taking away the need to increase local or state taxes.

Many of the city's citizens were all too willing to show their support for FDR. Over a million of them had benefited directly at various times of the decade from the policies of the New Deal. Housing programs, Social Security, public works projects, labor reform: These were measures for which many voters were directly grateful to Roosevelt and the Democrats. There was a more immediate reason for gratitude,

A panorama of Chicago in 1938. The next year Chicagoans delivered their verdict on the Democrats' war against poverty: They reelected Mayor Kelly, but by a narrow majority that reflected distrust of the Democrat party machine.

too: Shortly before the election Roosevelt announced $18 million in federal funds for the construction of a subway in the city.

Although Kelly won the election, victory was not as overwhelming as it might have been. The New Deal had run out of steam. The approaching war in Europe confused purely domestic considerations for voters. Kelly got high levels of the vote among ethnic and working-class communities but lost out in more affluent areas where people owned their own homes. Green received nearly 45 percent of the votes. The Republican Party was far from dead in Chicago. The election also demonstrated the support for the Democratic Party among black and poor voters, some of the chief beneficiaries of the New Deal.

Economic security had become the most important determinant in politics, and the war would soon deliver it. Politics remained concerned with philosophical questions about the size, power, and role of federal government. The debate was a complicated one. In Chicago, at least, a growth in federal spending had paradoxically led directly to the increased strength of the local political organization.

SEE ALSO

◆ Volume 1, Chapter 7, Hoover: The Search for a Solution

◆ Volume 2, Chapter 2, The First Hundred Days

◆ Volume 2, Chapter 4, Where Did the Depression Bite?

◆ Volume 2, Chapter 5, Putting People to Work

◆ Volume 4, Chapter 5, Welfare

◆ Volume 5, Chapter 3, Society in the 1930s

2

SHADOW OVER THE COUNTRYSIDE

Many farmers had struggled financially before the Depression made things worse in the early thirties. Roosevelt's New Deal helped the development of large "agribusiness," further worsening the plight of the small farmer.

America's economy had been faltering in fits and starts for more than a decade before the stock-market crash of 1929 (see Volume 1, Chapter 5, "The Fantasy World"). Many farmers had been experiencing financial hardships before the Depression, and few had any savings, having spent any money they possessed on farm maintenance and investing in land and new machinery. Furthermore, although they were relatively self-sufficient in terms of food, they received little, if any, financial aid from the government.

The biggest problem facing farmers in the early years of the Depression was the very low pricing of agricultural products. Farm prices had fallen steeply in 1920 after the end of World War I in Europe in 1918. Farm income had dropped

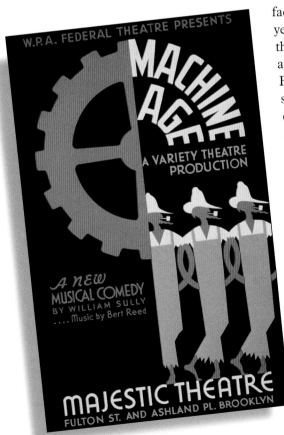

Poster for a Federal Theater Project presentation of Machine Age, *a musical comedy by William Sully, showing three farmers standing next to a cog from a machine. While new farm machinery enabled many farm owners to run their farms more efficiently, it put huge numbers of farm laborers out of work.*

from almost $17 billion in 1919 to less than $9 billion in 1921. In 1929 the purchasing power of agricultural produce was still only 91 percent of what it had been before World War I.

Farming had long been the backbone of the nation, even though industrialization since the late 19th century had increasingly shifted the nation's economic energy away from agriculture. Farming, however, had a tradition of economic instability, caused by the cycles of nature as well as by commodity pricing. The Depression increased this instability.

Farmers increasingly asked for federal intervention. After all, they argued, government attention was being paid to assisting other businesses and industries. Agriculture had been all but neglected by government officials early in the century. In the 1920s legislative issues of interest to farmers included credit for agriculture, the formation of farmer cooperatives, and agricultural exports. During the Coolidge administration farmers received no aid from the chief executive, leaving Congress to fulfill that role. Attempts made between 1924 and 1928 to get government

At a famous 1932 speech to farm leaders in Topeka, Kansas, in the center of the corn belt, Roosevelt spoke about his plans to bring in a far-reaching program to assist the nation's farmers.

to support farmers' incomes were vetoed. In 1929 Herbert Hoover's Agricultural Marketing Act created the Farm Board to fund agricultural cooperatives whose members agreed to reduce production in order to raise farm prices. The plan was a failure, however, and wasted a great deal of government money.

By the time Franklin Roosevelt entered the White House in March 1933, the nation's agriculture was in a perilous condition. In the Hundred Days that launched his presidency, the many difficulties facing farmers took second priority only to the immediate banking crisis (see Volume 2, Chapter 2, "The First Hundred Days").

There were many reasons why the farm population should be uppermost in Roosevelt's mind. In 1933 agriculture still employed 30 percent of the workforce, and the farmers of the South and the West,

with a tradition of progressive politics behind them, had formed one of the most solidly pro-Democratic constituencies at the 1932 election. Burdened by heavy debts and suffering from rock-bottom agricultural prices, farmers looked for a quick return on their electoral investment in the party.

1. FARMERS' PROBLEMS CONTINUE TO GROW

What had changed beside the times? There were more people living in the United States, and entrepreneurial farmers wanted to feed them as well as export surplus. They also wanted to take advantage of new technology in the form of mechanized equipment such as combines and tractors. Their land holdings also grew. "Agriculture's paradigm [a typical model] changed from widespread subsistence farming to a system of farms providing food for the newly urbanized areas," according to a U.S. Senate report. "In 1890 roughly four of five Americans lived in rural areas. By 1915 only 65 percent were living outside cities of 30,000 or more.

Farming's Golden Age

Farmers had experienced their best years ever immediately before and during World War I (1914–1918). The period from 1910 to 1914 is sometimes referred to as farming's "golden age." During the war American farmers increased production to compensate for the devastation of European farming, as well as to feed the Allied forces. In addition, growing numbers of people were living in the United States as a result of immigration. Farm prices rose, but costs—such as for new machinery and labor—were also high. Still, farmers were making 50 percent more money than other workers in the years 1918 and 1919. After the war the surplus U.S. farmers had created to feed so many was no longer needed. Foreign agriculture began to recover; most nations were no longer able to pay for American products. The gross income of farmers dropped $4 billion in 1920. During the Depression the golden age between 1910 and 1914 came to be the basis of comparison when computing parity prices.

From 1860 to 1900 the average size of American farms had declined from 199 acres to 147 acres, and the percentage of farmers in the labor force had declined from 58 to 38 percent."

Three Types of Farming

There were three very different agricultural class structures that varied by region during the thirties. They were family farming in the Midwest, industrial-capitalist farming—also in the Midwest and throughout the West—and the remaining vestiges of the plantation system throughout the South. In the West most farmers were landowners, while in the South many were sharecroppers—they did not own the land they farmed, but gave part of what they grew to their landowner for rent. The move from small farms to "factory farming" was the first sign of the decline of family farms and the emergence of what became known as agribusiness. As one California grower put it, "We no longer raise wheat here, we manufacture it."

COMPETITION FROM ABROAD

There were many other factors that hampered the profitability of agriculture. Those nations unaffected by the war in Europe were now competing with the United States in foreign markets. The competition included commodities grown in the newly formed Soviet Union. Because American farmers needed to pay for the new equipment they had purchased as well as other increasing costs, they continued to produce as much as they could, even when they knew that the surplus they were creating would drive prices for their produce lower. This meant they needed more land for more crops.

PROBLEMS OF MACHINERY

Machinery, although it allowed farmers to be more efficient, could be an expensive trap. As

A new piece of farm equipment in action in Carson County, Texas. Buying farm machinery was a major expense for the farmer, who had quite likely already gone into debt to buy more land on which to use it. Consequently he found himself needing to increase production to recoup his costs.

tractors and other equipment became more affordable, farmers sought to increase their land holdings. If they went into debt to buy more land and equipment, they had to produce more goods by growing more corn or wheat or raising more hogs, say. If they could not produce more goods, or if commodity prices were low, the consequences could be dire.

•

"We no longer raise wheat here, we manufacture it."

•

Large farmers were at greater risk, since large farms required more equipment, which was expensive. Paradoxically, smaller farmers succumbed more rapidly to financial instability, having less capital to fall back on.

Mechanization made it possible for fewer people to do the same work. As farms grew in size, they

Debts Rise as Prices Fall

Farm mortgage debt rose from $3.2 billion in 1910 to $9.6 billion by 1930, which eventually led to large-scale foreclosures. In that same period the total number of farms had dropped by 71,000. There was a marked reduction in farm prices between 1929 and 1932. Farm income had dropped 50 percent between 1929 and 1930. Commodity prices were being cut as the cost of living dropped. People no longer had money to spend, even on basic items.

needed less manual labor. Farm size increased from 139 acres in 1910 to 157 acres in 1930. A few combines could harvest grain much more quickly and efficiently than a team of threshers. As a result more and more people at the subsistence income levels were displaced and unemployed.

FARM FORECLOSURES

In 1931, with bank failures increasing and farmland dried out or sterile, no one wanted to buy the land farmers tried to sell to pay their debts. Prices continued to fall. Farmers unable to keep up with their mortgage payments were foreclosed on in record numbers. Foreclosure was the

A farm foreclosure sale in Iowa in 1932. Between 1927 and 1932 thousands of small farmers, unable to meet their mortgage payments, were evicted from their farms.

process by which banks and other mortgage holders evicted farmers unable to keep up the payments on their properties. The banks usually tried to sell the farm to recover a little of their original mortgage loan and sold off the farmer's equipment and livestock at auction.

In the five years between 1927 and 1932 as many as 10 percent of farms had been foreclosed. On a single day in April 1932, according to one account, fully one-quarter of Mississippi state's farmland was sold at auction.

Neighbors often rallied behind each other in these instances. There are numerous stories about mortgage holders more happy to take what little funds neighbors were able to gather in these so-called "penny auctions" than to face potential violence from angry farmers. One story tells of an agent for a mortgage holder threatened with lynching if he did not comply with demands to pay a family fair market value for their livestock and

equipment. Frustration was growing, and nowhere greater than in the Midwest and Plains states. As he stumped for reelection in 1932 William "Wild Bill" Langer,

•

"Shoot the banker if he comes on your farm. Treat him like a chicken thief."

•

governor of North Dakota, urged constituents to "Shoot the banker if he comes on your farm. Treat him like a chicken thief."

Farmers were in angry mood. Roosevelt took office to the sound of the powerful Farmers' Holiday Association calling for a national farm strike if Washington did not provide early and substantial relief. The association was doing nothing

H. F. Walling, drought chairman, was a farmer and a member of the Farmers' Holiday Association, which campaigned for better terms for farmers by organizing strikes.

more than reflecting the growing tendency of farmers to take matters into their own hands.

In the fight against foreclosures the farmers banded together to intimidate prospective purchasers of their property and to prevent the courts from issuing foreclosure orders in the first place. Violent behavior occurred in many states. In Wisconsin dairy farmers dumped their milk on the roadsides and scuffled with sheriffs. A group of striking ranchers in Nebraska forced a freight train to stop and removed its cargo of cattle.

One of the most violent of incidents happened in Iowa. Farmers barged into a courtroom and interrupted a judge presiding over a mortgage hearing. The men grabbed him and drove him out of town. They reportedly debated

Many debt-ridden farmers, having been evicted from their farms, saw their few remaining possessions sold at auction.

Congress Helps Farmers with Debts

Congress passed the Emergency Farm Mortgage Act of 1933 and the Farm Mortgage Refinancing Act of 1934 to help farmers with their debts. The Federal Farm Mortgage Corporation, created by the 1934 act, was given a fund of $2 billion. It had the authority to remortgage farms at much lower rates of interest—making it easier for farmers to meet payments—to provide federal money for new mortgage loans, and to settle farmers' debt repayments on equitable terms. Within 18 months one-fifth of all farm mortgages had been refinanced on better terms for the farmer.

how they would punish him: Lynching? Dragging him behind a car? They ultimately stripped him and dumped grease on his head.

Farmers' Strike

Growing unrest eventually led to a farmers' strike in the summer of 1932, led by Milo Reno, a sometime Iowa minister. Reno, once described as "one of the most effective evangelical speakers that a long tradition of rural protest had ever produced," was president of the Iowa Farmers' Union, a more militant organization than other agricultural groups such as the Grange and American Farm Bureau Federation. Farmers could not strike in the same way as employees of corporations or organizations because they had no employer to strike against, so they devised a different form of action. They would put a halt to selling their produce and livestock, thus causing a shortage until prices increased enough to cover the costs of production. This plan

Iowa Bans Further Foreclosures

The Iowa legislature was the first to act against the growing frustration and emotional toll foreclosures were exacting on residents across the state. In 1933 Iowa enacted legislation designed to place a moratorium on any further mortgage foreclosures. Days later the state of Minnesota followed suit; soon more states were enacting similar legislation. These measures did stave off some foreclosures but often did not apply to foreclosures already in progress or to mortgages that had been used to buy goods or equipment.

food and milk spilled and destroyed. The largest blockades were on the highways between Omaha, Nebraska, and Council Bluffs, Iowa. Tension was palpable. Both strikers and officials armed themselves. Despite the fact that both sides had weapons at hand, however, the threat of violence remained greater than acts of violence. In an incident outside Sioux City, Iowa, one person was killed and five injured. The strike itself was not as effective as organizers had hoped: Despite their widespread concerns, fewer than 10 percent of the farmers in the Midwest actually participated in the strike.

FEARS OF GROWING UNREST

The potential for violence was growing more alarming. Agitation, observers feared, would boil over and manifest itself in widescale violence and property damage. On January 25, 1933, the president of the American Farm Bureau Federation, traditionally the most conservative of the farm organizations, warned legislators: "Unless something is done for the American farmer we will have revolution in the countryside within less than 12 months." Midwestern governors met with Roosevelt that year to explain the situation and voice their concerns that unrest might escalate.

gave rise to the Farmers' Holiday Association. Just like a bank holiday in finance, the farmers were going to take time off from buying or selling. The action was scheduled to start on July 4, 1932, but was delayed until August.

The holiday strike was intended to last for a month, but it went on longer than anticipated. In areas from Wisconsin to Nebraska armed picketers set up roadblocks to halt transportation of any farm products. Trucks were seized and

Farmer John Barnett and his family, struggling to survive on their farm in around 1935. Growing anger in the farming community at the government's inability to organize adequate relief led to outbreaks of violence.

A supply of surplus corn in Saline County, Illinois. Overproduction drove commodity prices so low that farmers and the government tried to store surpluses to create shortages and increase prices.

A journalist who set out to travel east across country from the Carolinas in 1932 reported seeing "fields of unpicked cotton that tell a mute story of more cotton than could be sold for enough, even, to pay the cost of picking. Vineyards with grapes still unpicked, orchards of olive trees hanging full of rotting fruits, and oranges being sold at less than the cost of production." It was not only arable farming that was in crisis. A congressional subcommittee heard evidence of ranchers in the West who, unable to market their sheep, were slitting the throats of whole flocks and flinging the carcasses away.

THE MIGRATION PROBLEM

Dwindling work, coupled with droughts through the midwestern United States between 1920 and 1929, set the stage for an exodus from rural America. An estimated six million people fled rural areas through the 1920s. This continued into 1930, when about two million people left farming areas. Farmers who had lost their land through drought, debt, or both, and tenant farmers and farm laborers whose jobs had become

•

"…more cotton than could be sold for enough, even, to pay the cost of picking."

•

redundant due to the increasing use of farm machinery, abandoned their homes. Many rural Southerners migrated to the industrial cities in search of work.

AGRICULTURAL SURPLUSES

The economic problems of the early 1930s were exacerbated by agricultural surpluses. The root of the crisis, in the eyes of the New Dealers, was that massive overproduction was driving down prices, particularly for the four prime crops of the nation: cotton, corn, wheat, and tobacco. Volun-tary reductions in production did not work. Between 1929 and 1933 U.S. industry had responded to the onset of depression by cutting back production by more than 40 percent; agricultural output had fallen by only 6 percent. Farmers continued to plant despite the fact that prices were falling. They were afraid to stop in case the farmer next door kept planting and prices went up again. Besides, wasn't the point of farming to grow as much as one could in any given season? Many people began to see government regulation as the only way to break the cycle of overproduction.

In the closing years of the 1920s about 600,000 people a year moved from the South into the crowded towns and cities. There, many found themselves victims of another blight, unemployment.

By 1932 many white Americans were going "back to the land." The farm population grew by 6.3 percent between 1930 and 1935. By 1935 an estimated 33 million people lived on farms. Sociologists explained the trend as a return to a pastoral life after hard times in the cities. The real reason was much simpler: There was no work in the cities. Black sharecroppers who had emigrated from the South, however, could not return home: They remained stuck in the city.

Farmers Better Off at Home

Not all historians paint the plight of rural Americans in dark colors. "Many farm families were spared the devastation the 1929 stock market crash caused so many others," explained the *Countryside & Small Stock Journal,* because they did not have any stocks: "Most farmers… had their homes, and a food supply. Most were also self-sufficient in terms of energy, because…electrical power had not yet reached most of the country-side." The writer did acknowledge that some farmers were suffering, however: "As always, there were exceptions. Tenants were frequently displaced, and farmers who had gone into debt for land or machinery often lost it all. But in general, farm life was much better than city life…. So when the banks closed and the soup

An abandoned tenant house in Hall County, Texas. Many tenants forced off the land by poverty or mechanization made their way to towns and cities; urban poverty, in turn, drove many back to the country.

kitchens opened, those self-sufficient people went about their lives with very little change."

2. HOOVER AND THE FARM BOARD

Hoover's administration created the Farm Board in 1929. Its purpose was to fund agricultural cooperatives whose members

A homeless family of tenant farmers in 1936. During the Depression many tenant farmers were displaced and forced to seek work elsewhere.

voluntarily agreed to reduce production or withhold products from the market. Government also bought large quantities of the

A wagon being loaded with sheaves of wheat in Frederick County, Maryland, in June 1937. The AAA subsidized the export of surplus wheat, mainly to China.

four staple crops in an effort to raise agricultural prices without restricting production levels by reducing the huge farm surpluses. The net effect of these programs was worse than none. Farm income remained static, and the value of farmland dropped by $25 million. The government, meanwhile, spent $360 million without raising prices.

Like other elements of the breakdown of the economy in the early part of the Depression, the crisis in farming posed a larger question about the very nature of capitalism (see Volume 4, Chapter 1, "Left vs. Right"). The laws of supply and demand on which a free-market economy was based did not seem to offer any way out of the crisis. While children went to school in rags, fields of cotton went unpicked. People starved while

food rotted. A traveler observed that "while Oregon sheep raisers fed mutton to the buzzards, I saw men picking for meat scraps in the garbage cans in...New York and Chicago." Similar questions about the politics of food distribution remain common to many financially undeveloped and developing nations.

3. NEW DEAL FARM REFORMS

What was wrong with the economic system that it allowed such suffering to occur in a land of plenty? FDR and his advisors were obliged to consider the question and to decide whether radical solutions were available.

The language of Roosevelt's inaugural address on March 4, 1933, was indeed radical. "Plenty is at our doorstep," he stated, "but a generous use of it languishes in the very sight of supply. Primarily this is because rulers of the exchange of mankind's goods have failed through their own stubbornness and their own incompetence,

have admitted their failure and have abdicated."

American business was not used to such hostile language from a president, but economic circumstances took the ground from under them. It helped the new president, as he considered the state of the rural economy, that agriculturalists and business leaders were, by and large, of one mind. The men who ran banks and insurance companies, retail outlets and mail-order firms, all knew that their prosperity was endangered by the collapse of rural purchasing power. There was, therefore, little protest in Congress or in the country when Roosevelt announced that he was abandoning his original intention of adjourning Congress after securing the initial passage of measures to stabilize the banking system. The agricultural crisis was too pressing to allow an adjournment (see Volume 2, Chapter 2, "The First Hundred Days").

Previous administrations—most notably the Coolidge administration from 1925 to 1929—had

An African American sharecropper plows a field ready for planting cotton in 1934. The man had farmed the poor, grassy land in North Carolina for four years. Sharecroppers, along with tenant farmers and laborers, were on the bottom rung of the agrarian ladder and often the last to receive aid—despite being the most in need.

for the most part ignored agricultural issues (see Volume 1, Chapter 5, "The Fantasy World"). The Roosevelt administration took a greater interest in addressing farmers' needs. New Deal farm reform began as a necessity. The economic problems confronting farmers were, it was felt, so complex that they could not be resolved in a free-market economy.

The responsibility for finding a solution to farming's difficulties lay with Secretary of Agriculture Henry Wallace (1888–1965) (see box, page 36). He and his advisors had to deal with two different problems. One was the immediate need to raise the prices of agricultural products and ease the credit and mortgage burden on farmers. The other, more deep-seated problem was the persistence of rural poverty even in times of

prosperity. For decades, even in years like 1929 that were good for the economy as a whole, there had been little prosperity for farmers except for the few involved in large-scale agribusiness.

DOMESTIC ALLOTMENT PLAN
In 1933 Wallace focused on the immediate financial crisis facing farmers. His stated objective was to restore parity between agricul-

ture and industry by what was called a "domestic allotment" plan. The core idea of the scheme was to restrict the amount of land under cultivation and to pay compensation to farmers who agreed to limit their production; the money would come from a tax on the processors of agricultural produce, like millers, canners, packers, and distributors.

Enabling Bill
Roosevelt insisted that any bill put before Congress be framed in extensive consultation with farming representatives and that any recommendations for action would have to receive their approval. Some farm leaders were opposed to restricting the acreage under cultivation; they favored dumping surpluses abroad at low prices in order to raise farmers' incomes. Roosevelt was implacably opposed to dumping, however. After a pleasing series of meetings with Wallace, the farmers' representatives were ready

Boom-Bust Cycles

Among the difficulties facing farmers in the early thirties were the pronounced boom-bust cycles that are endemic in agriculture. A part of the explanation lies in the nature of nature; it cannot be controlled. Because the price of food does not affect the amount consumed—people have to eat, but they will not eat more because prices are lower—this exacerbates the problem. If there is plenty of produce in the market, people cannot and will not buy the surplus, despite low prices. The result is that farm incomes are variable year to year and wholly unstable. Manufacturers can adjust supply; farmers cannot. One of the reasons government became involved in agriculture was to try and counter these fluctuations.

Henry Wallace

Henry Wallace, secretary of agriculture from 1933 to 1940, was raised in a political family. His father had held the same post under Roosevelt's Republican predecessors, Warren Harding and Calvin Coolidge. Wallace was an intellectual with a deep knowledge of farming, an economist, and a breeder whose experiments in breeding hybrid corn had brought him to the attention of the farming community. He was also the editor of a magazine called *Wallace's Farmer*. His shy manners masked a determination to get his way and get things done. He had a quirky mystical side, but his strong religious faith underlay his hatred of unemployment.

Wallace belonged to the Jeffersonian agrarian tradition, which envisioned farm planning in order to provide food for society and ensure stability for farmers. He was the driving force behind the involvement of farmers in the creation of agricultural policy and an advocate of paying farmers to restrict production. He was responsible for various programs, including soil conservation, providing warehouses for surplus crops, and assisting tenant farmers. His liberalism endeared him to a powerful section of the Democratic Party, and FDR chose him as his running mate for the 1940 presidential election. After serving as vice-president, Wallace ran as the unsuccessful candidate of the Progressive Party in the presidential election of 1948.

Secretary of Agriculture Henry Wallace addresses farmers from Vermont and New Hampshire in 1937.

to barter. Speed was essential. Any new plan would have to be in place before the planting season. Wallace and the farm leaders came to a quick agreement by fudging the issue. They agreed on an enabling bill that gave Wallace the discretion to choose from a number of options designed to raise prices, in addition to the allotment plan. He could negotiate agreements by which processors agreed to pay farmers minimum prices; he could buy up and store cotton, like the Hoover Farm Board; he could pay subsidies to farmers for exports. There was no guarantee, however, that the new policy, by weakening the emphasis on the restriction of cultivation, would answer the pressing need to reduce agricultural surpluses.

THE AAA
Pressure remained on the Roosevelt administration. During a special session in March 1933, called to address the banking emergency, the president asked Wallace to call a farm leaders' conference to reach a consensus on legislation. Their consensus would become the basis of the Agricultural Adjustment Act, often referred to as AAA or Triple A. Roosevelt saw this legislation as "the trial of a new means to rescue agriculture." In early April the act passed easily through the House of Representatives without amendment. Conservative sen-

Farmers and farm laborers stand in line to collect their surplus commodities. The AAA authorized the distribution of surplus food to those in need.

ators, alarmed at Roosevelt's decision to interfere so boldly in the free operation of the agricultural market, and sympathetic also to the processors' fury at being asked to foot the bill, were less inclined to hurry the bill through the Senate.

Their hand was forced by outbreaks of renewed violence from farmers in the Corn Belt. When the Farmers' Holiday Association called for a national farmers' strike for May 13, the Senate was brought to heel. The AAA was approved by the Senate and signed on May 12, 1933, averting the strike. In addition to production adjustment programs, the AAA also authorized a number of marketing agreements and licenses, which were designed to

promote the orderly marketing of perishable commodities that could not be stored, and organized the distribution of surplus food to school-lunch programs and to people in need.

Restoring Farmers' Purchasing Power
The Department of Agriculture estimated in 1932 that farmers' purchasing power was half of what it had been in the "Golden Age"

Milburn Wilson

The voluntary "domestic allotment" plan, the cornerstone of agricultural policy during the New Deal, was not the brainchild of any one person. However, the chief credit for the idea went to a professor of economics at Montana State College, Milburn Wilson. Throughout the 1920s Wilson had been unable to devise any means of improving farm prices so long as overproduction of crops persisted. He came to the conclusion, after a visit to the wheat farms of the Soviet Union, that there was little point in American wheat farmers continuing to produce higher yields of grain per acre. American wheat farmers would never, he believed, be able to compete with Soviet farmers, whose lower costs and larger farms gave them a

decisive edge in world markets. He therefore reached the conclusion that only by cutting production could farmers adapt to the needs of the American market. Wilson made it his business to lobby everyone of any importance in the farming world to try to persuade them that he had the answer to agriculture's problems. Two of the most important people whom he won over to his idea were Rexford Tugwell and Henry Wallace. Tugwell was a leading member of the "Brain Trust," which masterminded Roosevelt's 1932 election campaign, and Wallace was secretary of agriculture. Together the two men were to become the architects of agricultural policy throughout President Roosevelt's administration.

Food Assistance Programs

During the 1930s Congress created food assistance programs to help millions of people in poverty. Some of these programs, started by the New Deal, still exist in modified forms such as food stamps and programs to provide lunch and milk in schools. According to one Senate history, "Food assistance programs were aimed at diminishing the excess supply of farm products.... The high unemployment levels of the Depression created the paradox of hunger side-by-side with the low prices and mounting surpluses of farm products." In 1933 the Agricultural Adjustment Act organized the distribution of surplus food to poor households across the country. By 1939 nearly 13 million people were receiving food from the federal government. New Deal programs also aided schools in the organization, funding, and expansion of daily lunch programs for schoolchildren.

Schoolchildren benefit from a free school lunch thanks to the AAA, which authorized the distribution of surplus food to school lunch programs.

immediately before, during, and after World War I. The act had several components designed to restore farmers' purchasing power and stabilize prices. One was to cut production, which would eliminate surplus crops of the basic commodities; another was to establish parity prices. Parity was a mathematical calculation to guarantee commodity pricing, developed by the Department of Agriculture. First used in the 1920s, the idea was that government would base prices on the flush years of 1910 to 1914.

Destroying Surplus Crops
Responsibility for implementing the act lay with Henry Wallace and a new board, the Agricultural Adjustment Administration (AAA), headed by George Peek. Their first task was to destroy crops and slaughter livestock. Roosevelt had said, in reference to his program of farm relief, that he was in a race with the sun. He meant that farmers needed to have the relief measures in place, and to be receiving the benefits from them, before the sowing season began. Roosevelt was beaten by the sun. By the start of 1933 the amount of unsold cotton in the United States was greater than the average annual amount sold in world and domestic markets. Worse still, cotton farmers had planted an additional four million acres compared to the previous year.

Destruction of Crops
The AAA decided on an unprecedented course of action: the deliberate destruction of crops with payment to the affected farmers in compensation. Ten million acres of cotton were plowed up in the South at a cost to the government of about $200 million in benefit payments. The same strategy was applied to hog-farming. Low corn prices had stimulated overproduction of hogs at a time when the Depression generally had lowered demand for pork and bacon. The AAA therefore bought and slaughtered 8.5 million piglets and 200,000 sows. The spectacle horrified the public; the emergency measure was never repeated on such a large scale.

According to author Jake Goldberg, the elimination of surplus crops was "the cruelest part" of the government's agricultural programs. "Large amounts of milk, dairy products, and food grains were disposed of or allowed to rot," he writes. "The destruction of food during an economic depression, when the poor and the unemployed were going hungry, seemed irrational and caused a great deal of outrage. Secretary [Henry] Wallace carried out the destruction with great reluctance, but raising farm income was the priority and the surpluses had to be reduced."

Granting Farmers Subsidies

The federal government also established agricultural subsidies, which were granted to farmers who voluntarily reduced their acreage in production. Under the AAA farmers were to be paid direct benefits or rental payments. Also, this legislation provided loans to farmers to meet their mortgage payments. All these programs were to be funded by a production tax, but only on specific farm commodities.

Because the AAA provided price guarantees for voluntary crop reduction, those farmers who were already better off were able to profit, while poorer, small farmers continued to suffer. They included the sharecroppers, an estimated 75 percent of all the farmers in the South and Southwest, for example. In this way, the AAA was vital in quickening the development of large-scale agribusiness at the expense of family farms.

A FERA camp for unemployed women in Arcola, Pennsylvania, 1934. In addition to providing relief to those in need, FERA created numerous work projects, which were staffed by unemployed adults.

Success of the AAA

The early results of the government's farm program were encouraging. Agricultural income rose by 50 percent during Roosevelt's first term. However, some of this was due to droughts in the Great Plains (see Chapter 3, "The Dust Bowl"). Because there were lower quantities of commodities due to the bad weather, crops produced in other regions fetched

•

"The destruction of food during an economic depression... seemed irrational..."

•

higher prices. At the end of 1933 the price of cotton had risen from 6.5 cents a pound to 10 cents a pound, and the cash value of that year's crop was $114 million more than it would have been without

the new measures. Planters received more than $110 million in benefits and rental repayments for land left uncultivated. The price of hogs remained stagnant, but government purchase of pigs for slaughter increased hog farmers' income by 10 percent. Corn growers, too, benefited from contracts made with the AAA. Corn yields were lower than at any time since 1881, and benefits brought in $300 million of income. At the same time, under the government's new credit facilities corn growers, like cotton growers, were able to store surpluses and tide themselves over with low-interest loans until prices rose again. Wheat farmers had their incomes boosted in several ways. To benefit payments for cutting production levels were added subsidies on 28 million bushels of cheap exports, which went chiefly to China. The Farm Credit Administration also bought 16 million bushels to distribute to the poor.

The program had loopholes and disadvantages, especially with

A rural rehabilitation county agent talks to a client outside Hayward, California, in 1936. The main purpose of FERA's rehabilitation division was to provide loans to destitute farmers.

regard to finance. For example, the improved farm prices meant that cash-strapped U.S. consumers had to pay more for basic food items.

FERA

Another important piece of New Deal legislation was written during the First Hundred Days. The creation of the Federal Emergency Relief Administration (FERA) in 1933 was considered by some historians to have been the first truly significant federal government effort to alleviate poverty. Harry Hopkins, who had administered a similar program in New York while Roosevelt was governor of that state, headed the program. Immediately upon his appointment he authorized $5 million in grants to six states.

Critics said that Hopkins made up his policies on the fly.

When states failed to help those in need, Hopkins felt no compunction about cutting off federal funding. When Oklahoma officials, for example, failed to raise taxes on oil to pay for similar types of aid programs, Hopkins withheld funding and federalized aid in the state. Similar events transpired in other states, including New York, Louisiana, and Kentucky.

Rural Rehabilitation

Several special aid programs were created under the FERA umbrella, including a rural rehabilitation plan. The Rural Rehabilitation Division was established on April 1, 1934, primarily to make loans to destitute farm families. These loans enabled farmers to purchase basic necessities required to keep their operations viable, like livestock, equipment, seed, and fertilizer.

Although aid was supposed to be equitable, social and political

issues influenced how funds were distributed. Political pressure exerted on employees working at the local level was great, especially when state officials wanted a say in how the federal money was distributed. In a case in Massachusetts, for example, the state administrator was accused of diverting funds from the urban core of Boston, where residents were in dire need, into suburban areas where his friends lived. Race also affected aid distribution, especially in the rural South (see Volume 5, Chapter 2, "Equality for Some"). There was apparently also disparity between the purposes to which states allocated FERA aid grants to urban and rural areas. A report from Anderson County, Tennessee, recommended funding a vocational training program in rural areas but preference was given to the building of a public swimming pool instead.

Reports of these problems filtered back to Washington, D.C. Investigating what was going on was left to reporters such as Lorena Hickok and others, whom the administration dispatched to report on what they found across the country (see Volume 2, Chapter 4, "Where Did the Depression Bite?").

Farmers Want Compulsory Legislation

Despite signs of improvement, the fall of 1933 brought more agrarian discontent and a stiffening of farmers' radicalism. Part of the trouble was that larger farmers were receiving federal checks rather than sharecroppers and laborers. In part this reflected a general transition toward agribusiness, which had the effect of pushing out marginal farmers, but Black laborers in the South especially felt powerless against all-white AAA committees. There was also dissatisfaction with FDR's cautious approach. The AAA, for example, was not compulsory. Restrictions on production had to be mutually agreed between the farmer and the government. By the fall farmers—especially wheat growers in the

Midwest—were demanding compulsory measures for cutting production and fixing prices.

In retrospect the attitude of the wheat growers might appear surprising. In the summer of 1933, however, the West suffered the beginning of a drought that, unbeknown at the time, was to last for four years. The result was a sharp decline in the wheat yield. As the time for sowing the winter crop approached, wheat growers grew increasingly anxious about how much to plant. Cotton growers in the South joined the wheat growers' demand for compulsory legislation. When Roosevelt indicated that he was not prepared to go that far, many farmers rallied to the call of the Farmers' Holiday Association and went on strike.

The initiative passed to Senator John Bankhead of Alabama, who filed a bill in the Senate to make cotton quotas compulsory. When the government sent out a questionnaire to discover what planters thought of Bankhead's proposal, it had a surprise. More than four-fifths of those who responded were in favor; only 2

percent were opposed. The response ended George Peek's tenure at the AAA. He had been opposed to crop restriction and supported price deals and export subsidies for farmers. He and the government had been at loggerheads since his appointment, and in December he was replaced by Chester Davis, a champion of controlled production.

Bankhead's bill received congressional assent in April 1934. The Kerr-Smith Tobacco Control Act, passed at the urging of the tobacco growers, placed a heavy tax on the sale of tobacco by growers who had not signed

How rural rehabilitation could work: The family who lived in this one-room shack in Tulare County, California, received a loan of $50 to buy 20 acres of unimproved land. A further loan of $700 from the Farm Security Administration enabled them to purchase stock and equipment. From that start they went on to acquire seven cows, three sows, a homemade pumping plant, and 10 acres of improved permanent pasture.

Tennessee Valley Authority

Established in 1933 to create employment in a financially depressed region, the Tennessee Valley Authority (TVA) had several objectives of benefit to farmers (see Volume 2, Chapter 5, "Putting People to Work"): flood control; the planting of trees to shelter and protect the soil; the introduction of new ways of farming to make the nutrient-depleted soil rich again; and the manufacture of cheap fertilizers. This last reflected another important purpose of the TVA: to produce nitrogen for use in munitions.

New dams were built to control the Tennessee River. As well as preventing flooding, they also produced hydroelectricity. Previously only two out of every 100 farms in the region were supplied with electricity. The TVA sold its electricity cheaply, which gave farmers in the region access to affordable power to illuminate and modernize their homes.

The TVA's electricity was also used to make cheap fertilizers to rejuvenate exhausted soil. Other TVA programs involved planting trees on a huge scale all over the valley. In addition, farmers were encouraged to plant crops such as grass and clover, which would provide ground cover all year round. They were persuaded to practice contour plowing—plowing across hillsides, rather than up and down—to prevent rain running down the furrows and taking the soil with it.

From 1933 the TVA set up "test demonstration farms" in different areas of the valley. The owners of these farms agreed to practice new conservation methods. Neighboring farmers soon saw the benefits as crop yields increased, and soon more and more farmers were adopting conservation-friendly methods of farming.

A TVA chemical plant, with an electric furnace loaded with phosphate to make fertilizer, near Muscle Shoals, Alabama.

contracts to reduce production levels. A year later pressure from senators from Maine and Idaho led to a compulsory Potato Crop Act.

SEVERE DROUGHT

Its agricultural relief legislation largely in place, the Roosevelt administration was confronted by the worst drought since the accurate recording of rainfall levels had begun 70 years earlier. Four years of drought, which reduced swathes of the West to a dust bowl, actually produced some welcome consequences for the government, notably in the form of a natural means of crop control. The wheat and corn programs initiated by the government, which were threatening to fail because of the number of farmers who refused to sign contracts with the AAA, instead now met their targets. The effect on cattle ranching was also dramatic. Beef farmers had been

A dead longhorn steer in Sioux County, Nebraska, victim of the drought in 1934.

among the most stubborn opponents of the government's scheme; however, unable now to buy enough grain to feed their herds, they sought the protection of the AAA in increasing numbers as the dry seasons continued. By the end of 1935 the government had bought some 8.5 million head of cattle for slaughter, and farmers and ranchers had agreed to cut their herds by 20 percent by the end of 1937.

REFORM OF RURAL SOCIETY

Neither the government nor the AAA, preoccupied as they were with the pressing and immediate task of reviving the agricultural economy, gave much thought to a fundamental reform of rural society. Some liberal officials, however, saw the crisis as a chance to seek a permanent rise in status and standard of living for those at the bottom of the ladder. Chester Davis, for example, the head of the AAA, insisted that the

1935 contracts for crop control among cotton planters include a clause compelling every landlord to retain the same number of tenant farms as he had rented out in 1933. However, Davis blocked the efforts of more radical members of the AAA to make landlords keep the same tenants.

DEMISE OF THE AAA

Despite the success of the AAA, it was short-lived, mainly as a result of political opposition. In 1936 the Supreme Court ruled it unconstitutional. A new

Agricultural Ajustment Act in 1938 created a second AAA in its place (see Chapter 6, "Continuing Plight of the Farmer," Volume 2, Chapter 6, "The Election of 1936," and Volume 4, Chapter 2, "The Supreme Court").

Racist Landlords

Despair stirred radical impulses among farm laborers and sharecroppers, the propertyless working class of rural society, in the summer of 1934. The Southern Tenant Farmers' Union, established in Arkansas in July under socialist leadership, was remarkable for bringing whites and blacks together in one movement. For their pains, however, the farmers were subjected to a campaign of anti-union terrorism by landlords who hunted down union members, shooting some of them and persuading sheriffs to arrest them in numbers. The white propertied class of Arkansas looked with contempt on the efforts of the poor to improve their lot and raise their status in rural society. "We have had a pretty serious situation here," one Arkansan told a *New York Times* reporter in the spring of 1935, "what with the mistering of the niggers and stirring them up to think the Government was going to give them forty acres."

3

THE DUST BOWL

By the 1930s human and climatic factors turned the Great Plains into a dusty wilderness whose inhabitants learned to live with poverty. Farmers left the land, hastening the transition from an agricultural to an industrial economy. The government, meanwhile, accepted the need for agricultural planning.

YEARS OF DUST

RESETTLEMENT ADMINISTRATION
Rescues Victims
Restores Land to Proper Use

Drought and erosion turned the soil of the southern Plains states to dust. The winds whipped up great dust storms, called rollers, that devastated the livelihoods, health, and family life of thousands of rural communities.

1. WHERE WAS THE DUST BOWL?

The area commonly indicated by the term Dust Bowl comprised some 97 million acres spread over 18 counties in southeastern Colorado, western Kansas, northeastern New Mexico, and the panhandles of Oklahoma and Texas. The region covered about 400 miles from north to south and 300 miles from east to west, with its center around Liberal in the southwest corner of Kansas, close to the Oklahoma state line.

The reach of the Dust Bowl extended far beyond this central area, however. Light dust was found as far west as Utah and north into Nebraska, and all of Kansas, Oklahoma, and Texas were covered in dust at one time or

A Resettlement Administration poster by artist Ben Shahn (1898–1969) depicts a striking image of the thirties: A farmer sits helplessly on his porch as a dust storm envelops his farm.

another. Such was the magnitude of many of the dust storms that their effect was felt even further away. In February 1936 red snow fell in New England. Its coloration was caused by Oklahoma dust that had blown 2,000 miles from the Great Plains to the East Coast. Housewives on the eastern seaboard learned to recognize the red dust from Oklahoma as they swept up topsoil from the Plains. One dust storm, in May 1934, blotted out the sun for five hours in New York City, Baltimore, and Washington, D.C. Dust even settled on the president's desk in the White House. In the Atlantic Ocean ships' crews speculated on the origin of the dust that covered their decks.

ORIGINS OF THE DUST BOWL

Many historians have traditionally blamed the Plains farmers for creating the dust that caused the storms. They argue that during the 1920s, farmers switched from growing a variety of crops to

concentrate solely on wheat production, thus damaging the network of roots that held the soil in place. Increased mechanization, meanwhile, brought larger acreages of land under the plow. When the rains failed to come in 1932, the conditions were right for turning soil to dust.

While this account is broadly accurate, the creation of the Dust Bowl was more complex. The

A photograph of the great storm that began on April 14, 1935, and spread right across Colorado, Kansas, and Texas to Oklahoma, where this picture was taken.

fragile ecosystem of the Plains had originally been misunderstood by the homesteaders who flooded into the region during the latter part of the 19th century. Much of the damage had already been done by the turn of the century.

HOMESTEADERS

When early homesteaders arrived from the east following the Homestead Act of 1862 to claim the 160 acres of land each was allowed, drought conditions and dust storms were already part of the environment. A severe drought in 1855 had dried up rivers and caused so much dust to blow that black snow was reported in Ohio. Damage to the soil had already started to occur because of overgrazing by sheep and cattle brought into the area by ranchers.

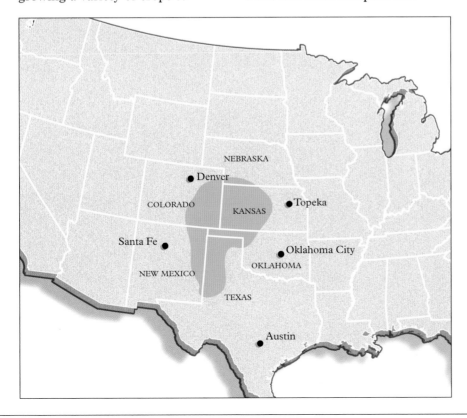

This map shows the main region covered by the Dust Bowl of the mid-1930s, which affected some 97 million acres in 18 counties across five main states.

Daniel Freeman, the "first homesteader," settled in Beatrice, Nebraska, in 1863.

VULNERABLE LANDSCAPE

The landscape of the Great Plains is historically more susceptible to the weather than most other regions in the nation. The thousands of acres of almost flat, grassy plains, unprotected by trees or other natural buffers, are exposed to erosion and destruction by the wind, sun, insects, and small prairie animals. The region is semiarid; years of rain are typically followed by years of drought. Even in years of average rainfall the wind and sun cause much of

A family in Nebraska on their way to their new home. The Homestead Act of 1862 permitted any citizen over the age of 21—including women, which was unusual at the time—to claim 160 acres of public land, on condition they improved it and settled there for five years.

the rain to evaporate before it is absorbed into the ground. Insects, rodents, and rabbits all increase in numbers during extended dry periods due to a reduction in predators; they destroy the plains grasses by overgrazing.

When the homesteaders arrived and saw thousands of acres of grass carpeting the plains, they reasoned that if grass could grow so well, then other crops should be equally successful. This fateful decision ultimately led to the Dust Bowl storms of the 1930s.

NEW WAYS OF FARMING

The soil of the Dust Bowl varies dramatically not only from state to state or county to county, but from town to town. Such is the soil variety in the region that soil types are named for their nearest town: Dumas and Sunray are two soil types named after towns.

Homesteaders from the East did not understand the farming techniques required in the region. The Department of Agriculture was founded in 1862 partly to help them learn how to adapt to the

new conditions. The homesteaders set about farming but found the grassy land impossible to break up.

The invention of the steel plow in the late 1800s allowed the homesteaders to break apart and turn over the sod, exposing the powdery soil beneath. Another invention, barbed wire, allowed them to parcel off their land and stop cattle from invading. Barbed wire also prevented animals from escaping their enclosures and promoted overgrazing by trapping animals in a confined space.

PLAINS POPULATION BOOM

The coming of the railroads brought a boom to the area, and thousands of homesteaders poured into the Great Plains and started to plow. Between 1870 and 1910 the population of the Plains states grew from just over half a million to more than five million. Few other regions in the country experienced such rapid growth—and almost all the newcomers were farmers.

In a short space of time millions of acres of prairie were

transformed into farming land. Some years crops were good; other years brought drought and other disasters. Between 1873 and 1881 prairie fires, grasshopper plagues, and dust storms were reported. In 1889 and 1890 a widespread drought struck the Plains. Drought struck again between 1893 and 1896. Natural disasters were worsened by a series of economic depressions between the end of the century and 1900. Many settlers left, but others held on.

Between 1900 and 1930 the Plains received plenty of rain, which led to good harvests and an end to dust conditions. Between 1914 and 1923 the annual average rainfall was 28 inches, compared to a normal average of just under 17 inches.

THE DEMAND FOR WHEAT

The outbreak of World War I was beneficial to farmers, who had to increase production to feed the nation and its allies. Farmers in the Great Plains were encouraged to grow as much wheat as possible, instead of crops such as sorghum and corn. Such was the

demand from the rest of the country, as well as from war-torn Europe, that wheat reached a price of $1.50 a bushel. Farmers turned to the latest technology to increase production.

By 1913 tractors were cheap and small enough for the average farmer to buy. The early models were kerosene powered and could do the work of 17 men and 50 horses. In 1915 there were approximately 3,000 tractors in Kansas; by 1920 that figure had jumped to 17,177; when the Depression began in 1929, it had reached 66,275.

Mechanized equipment—which included not only tractors but also combine harvesters—further altered farming. Early combines could not harvest most sorghums, again encouraging farmers to switch to wheat. Once a farmer had invested in farm equipment for wheat, however, he could no longer afford to plant other crops in the same quantity as wheat. However, since wheat was the crop of the moment, most farmers did not expect this to present a problem.

In 1919 an area of virgin land three times the size of Rhode Island was plowed up in the Great Plains. Demand for wheat remained high into the early 1920s, and farmers bought all the land they could afford. Banks backed the development of large-scale agribusiness that promised sizable profits. Between 1925 and 1930 new farms established on the southern plains covered an area

Plains Grasses

The grasses that historically grew on the Great Plains, such as galleta, grama, buffalo, and wire grass, were fully adapted to their environment. In dry years some grasses became dormant, coming back to life only when it rained; other grasses grew tall or short depending on the availability of water. Grass roots create a fine, powdery soil. However, because there are many more roots on grass plants than other shrubs, they hold the soil together. The small, thin roots interconnect to form a tough matting of turf that is hard to break up.

The destruction wrought by the dust and wind can clearly be seen in this photograph of a farmstead in Dallam County, Texas, 1938.

seven times that of Rhode Island. Two-thirds of the farms grew exclusively wheat.

Throughout the 1920s farmers continued to produce above-average wheat harvests. They believed, as did most agricultural scientists, that mechanization and wheat had solved the difficulties of farming the Plains. Few people connected the winds for which the plains were known with soil erosion. Basic farming principles such as allowing soil to regenerate were ignored in the rush to meet the huge demand.

WHEAT PRICE FALLS

The market had already changed, however. Economically weak after World War I, European countries could not afford to pay for American wheat; they also began to

Suitcase Farmers

In 1926 in the state of Texas the success of the harvest using mechanized equipment encouraged outsiders to start investing in farming. Businessmen from the east started to buy up land that they farmed only during their vacations. They would plow up the land, plant it, and then return in time for harvesting with the combine. By 1930 more than half the farms in the southern Great Plains were owned by people who did not actually live on them.

grow their own again. Demand shrank. Wheat that cost $1.50 a bushel during the war fell to 52 cents as early as 1920. Optimistic farmers carried on producing bumper crops, expecting new markets to emerge. International trade was in depression, partly because of high U.S. tariffs on imports. Prices remained low. When the stock market crashed in 1929, they fell again, losing half their value.

Among the first to suffer were the so-called "suitcase farmers" (see box, left). Many lost their jobs as the Depression deepened and had to rely on their farms for an income. As they increased wheat production, prices fell further.

The heavy rains and killer blizzards of the fall and winter of 1930 to 1931 brought hardship to farmers, but nourished a bumper crop in July 1931. There was so much wheat that farmers piled it along roadsides and in fields. The price had fallen so low that farmers were going broke. Those who had other ways of making money abandoned their farms.

The summer of 1931 was hot and dry. Rain in September encouraged farmers to plant their wheat, but in the 1932 growing season a combination of drought and torrential rain led to a poor yield. The reduction in the wheat crop did not greatly increase prices, however: In July 1932 farmers got 30 cents a bushel, and in August the price had risen to 36 cents. By the summer of 1932 signs of drought were evident everywhere across the Plains. Dust had begun to swirl across fields of parched crops. Farmers planted in the fall, but the winter of 1932 to 1933 was dry.

DUST BOWL WEATHER

The climatic history of the Dust Bowl is one of extremes. Although the thirties are remembered for continuing drought, there were also floods, blizzards, and torrential rains. The drought of the 1930s actually began with a flood in September 1930. Torrential rains hit the Oklahoma panhandle and washed away topsoil along with bridges, leaving the

Above: Farmers in Oklahoma squat in the shade while their crops burn in the fields during a drought in August 1936.

Below: President Roosevelt talks to the family of Jon Anderson, victim of a drought in Julesburg, Colorado, from an open car in 1936.

rivers to flood. Roads and highways became impassable rivers of mud. In November north winds brought a freezing blizzard to the region that killed a farmer and his horse who became lost near Boise City, Oklahoma.

The immediate cause of the dust storms in the thirties was the recurring drought that hit the region every year from 1930 until 1939. Although there was rain most years during the decade, it generally fell with such ferocity and so infrequently that dried-out fields and rivers were unable to absorb the large volume of water. Flooding inevitably followed.

What made the effects of the droughts of the 1930s worse than those of previous droughts was the great plow-up of the Plains that had taken place in the meantime. The grass that anchored the soil had long gone, and the crops that farmers had planted in its place only held soil in place while it was wet enough. Once sufficient time had passed without good rain, the soil turned increasingly dusty and began to blow across the flat, open landscape.

During 1930 little rain fell across the whole nation; 1931 was dry in the Plains, and although some rain fell in 1932, it was insufficient. In 1933 day after day was sunny, and months went by without any rain falling on the Plains. By then farmers were planting seeds in soil that had turned to dust and smothered young shoots. When the rains failed again in 1934 and 1935, some families could endure the conditions no longer and left (see Chapter 4, "California in the 1930s").

THE DUST STORMS BEGIN
The dust storms began in 1933 and peaked in 1935. For the rest of the decade they were limited to

Grasshoppers, Worms, and Jack Rabbits

Along with drought and dust storms, Plains farmers faced other hazards. As early as 1930 grasshoppers and spiders started to destroy crops. By 1933 their numbers had increased massively, and whole fields of crops were being eaten. One farmer's wife remembered the arrival of grasshoppers in 1933: "We had a large garden.... Our neighbors said: 'The grasshoppers have come in, they've taken every leaf off our trees, they're even starting to eat the fenceposts.' I thought that was a joke. Well, the next day they moved on here, and they did line up on the fenceposts."

Grasshoppers continued to descend on the five-state Dust Bowl heartland and inflicted ex-

•

"...they've taken every leaf off our trees, they're even starting to eat the fenceposts."

•

tensive damage on the land. By 1936 there were so many grasshoppers that one local newspaper wrote: "When it is possible to locate the exact home address of the pesky creatures we are suggesting that that section of the nation be referred to as the grasshopper bowl, as the people have dubbed this country the 'dust bowl.'"

The next year the grasshopper invasion grew worse. One estimate put the number of grasshoppers per acre in Beaver County, Oklahoma, at 23,400. The governor of New Mexico asked the National Guard to help highway department employees, relief workers, and private citizens spread poison to kill the grasshoppers in Union County. Plants were set up across the county to mix arsenite with a combination of sawdust, molasses, and banana oil to produce a poison. In Baca County, Colorado, poison was brought in by the boxcar-load to five mixing plants. Seventy-eight trucks from the highway department, and many

A sugar-beet plant damaged by grasshoppers, 1939. Plagues of grasshoppers, combined with dust storms and drought, caused huge problems for the Dust Bowl farmers in the thirties.

private trucks, distributed the poison around the clock to try to halt the grasshopper invasion. Other Dust Bowl counties also adopted programs of rapid grasshopper poisoning.

Despite all the efforts to reduce the grasshopper population, it seemed as though little impact had been made. The *Texhoma Times* reported on September 23, 1937, that "...in every direction from Texhoma grasshoppers are thick and are reported as eating the wheat almost as fast as it comes through the ground."

In 1938 grasshoppers attacked again during the summer months with even more vigor than before. Renewed poisoning campaigns made little progress. Five separate flights of grasshoppers flew over the town of Clayton in Union County as they migrated from Colorado and Oklahoma. The highways across Baca County were slick with the bodies of thousands of dead grasshoppers.

In August the situation worsened when the grasshoppers were joined by a plague of army worms that invaded the grasslands of Sherman County, Texas. The worms got into houses and had to be swept out with a broom. Worse still, people were not sure how to get rid of them. As with other aspects of the Dust Bowl, the plague of grasshoppers and worms only returned to normal levels when the rains started to fall steadily in 1938.

Another animal invasion that exacerbated farmers' difficulties for much of the decade was that of jack rabbits. Unlike the grasshopper plague, there was one positive side to the jack-rabbit plague: The rabbits provided a good source of meat for many families for much of the Depression.

Why so many rabbits invaded the Dust Bowl is unclear. Scientists and farmers speculated that either the drought conditions improved breeding or the rabbits were searching for grass.

So prolific were the rabbits that local people set about trying to exterminate them by clubbing them to death. Almost every Sunday, particularly in winter in the southern High Plains, people gathered on local farms to take part in so-called rabbit drives. Local newspapers would announce where the next rabbit drive was to be held and invite people to attend: "Everyone who has a club of any kind is invited to participate in the drive."

Once enough people had assembled at a particular farm, they would form a large circle, up

•

"Grasshoppers…are reported as eating the wheat almost as fast as it comes through the ground."

•

to a mile in diameter. As the people walked toward the center, the rabbits would jump in front of them; as the circle got smaller, the rabbits were forced into snowfence pens where they were beaten to death. Guns could not be used on the drive because they were too dangerous.

The trade in rabbit meat became an important business. In 1931 residents of Hooker, Oklahoma, killed and shipped more than 5,000 rabbits to relief agencies in Kansas City. Such a shipment had little effect on the overall numbers of rabbits, however. They were so populous that it was not unusual to kill more than 2,000 on a single drive.

One farmer near Guymon, Oklahoma, spent most of the Dust Bowl years hunting rabbits. Not only did he keep his family supplied with meat, but he traded some rabbits and sold the remainder for fur and pet food, providing an income for his family.

Farmers sack mixed grasshopper poison to use on their farms to control the pest, Oklahoma City, Oklahoma, June 1937.

the spring months. When the rains finally returned in 1939, the dust storms ended.

On January 19, 1933, a cold north wind hit western Kansas and continued to blow for several days. The wind lifted sand across fields, damaging the young wheat. Craters formed in the plowed fields; and when the wind reached Dalhart, Texas, it created acres of sand dunes. That summer the crops failed completely.

On November 11, 1933, another dust storm hit the region, covering an area from Montana to the Great Lakes and south toward the lower Mississippi Valley in dust. The worst storm to date, its severity alarmed local people and alerted the rest of the country to the plight of America's breadbasket. The storm was like a black blizzard: As the wind increased to gale force, it started to lift tons of dry, loose topsoil from the fields, creating huge clouds that the wind sent swirling up into the sky. From a distance they looked like rain clouds; but when they discharged their load of dirt, dust, and sand, whole areas were transformed into lunar landscapes.

A GREAT STORM

By 1935 the severity of the storms was at its peak. On April 14 one of the worst rollers of the decade hit the Dust Bowl. At 3:00 P.M. 300 people were fishing and picnicking at Two Buttes Lake, Colorado, when they saw in the distance a huge black cloud rolling in from the north. A high-pressure system had moved into eastern Wyoming and started to

Large drifts of soil have piled up against this farmer's barn near Liberal, Kansas, March 1936.

head south, lifting up the dry Plains soil as it advanced. People rushed for their cars and tried to make for home before the roller hit, but it was traveling so quickly that many were stranded in total darkness. As it moved south, the cloud of dust, which reached a height of 1,000 feet, stretched in an unbroken mass from eastern Colorado to western Kansas.

A resident of Liberal, Kansas, Lila Lee King, recalled how scared she was: "I was sure I was going to die, and I can vividly recall the dust storm although I was only eleven at the time. We lit matches and held them before our faces and we couldn't see the light unless it was quite near."

It took the storm only one and a quarter hours to travel the 105

A farmer in Cimarron County, Oklahoma, raising a fence to prevent it from being buried beneath drifting sand, April 1936.

2. LIFE IN THE DUST BOWL

The dust storms affected people's lives in many negative ways. As they became more frequent in the mid-1930s, people's health began to suffer. Even wearing a mask over the mouth failed to keep out the dust. Soon a respiratory illness called dust pneumonia started to cause sickness and even deaths, particularly in southwest Kansas and southeast Colorado, where it was not unusual for families to lose two or more members to dust pneumonia. The symptoms included choking and coughing up black mucus. Scientific studies showed that the dust contained a high level of silica from the soil, which poisons the body in much the same way as lead, by weakening its resistance to disease and irritating the mucous membranes of the respiratory system.

Other respiratory illnesses like sinusitis, pharyngitis, laryngitis, and bronchitis also became commonplace. Children and older people were particularly susceptible to dust diseases. Epidemics of measles and strep throat made life even harder.

A young farmer's son shields his eyes from the dust in Cimarron County, Oklahoma, in 1936.

miles from Boise City, Oklahoma, to Amarillo, Texas. By the time it hit Amarillo, the dust cloud was estimated to tower 15,000 feet into the air. In Garden City, Kansas, rain mixed with dust, sending mud balls down to earth, while in Dodge City the wind speed hit 60 miles an hour.

In Baca County, Colorado, the great storm was the culmination of five days of blowing dust. Roads disappeared under dust and sand; one truck driver spent five and a half hours driving 50 miles. Many other motorists were stranded on the highways. Railroad lines closed as dust piled onto the tracks. Visibility was so poor that a rescue team sent to retrieve a stranded train itself became stranded for two days. In the Texas panhandle the Fort Worth and Denver Railroad service could only resume after snow plows removed the drifting dust from the tracks.

Schools in the area closed a month early for summer because board members were tired of shoveling dust out of classrooms each morning, and because the dust brought the threat of disease. Cattle died when they ate the dust that covered their pasture. Even birds were terrified by the storm; geese, ducks, and smaller birds flew ahead to escape the storm.

Cattle Slaughter

By the summer of 1933 the drought, heat, dust, and overgrazing in the plains were causing cattle to die of starvation and suffocation. In addition, elsewhere in the country a cattle surplus caused the price of beef to fall to its lowest level since 1899, only $3.63 per hundred-weight. The cattle ranchers could not feed or water their cattle, but the nationwide glut meant that there was no market for them. For many the only solution was to destroy whole herds. The Federal Surplus Relief Corporation acted as early as 1933 with loans to farmers to prevent this, but the problem of starving cattle persisted throughout the thirties. Although many cattle were relocated out of the Dust Bowl, it was a slow process. By the time ranchers and government agencies had devised a plan for feeding the remaining cattle and relocating or slaughtering other livestock, the rains had returned.

Dust Storm Procedure

When a duster hit, daylight was totally obliterated: Day turned into night. As darkening skies warned of an approaching storm, people followed a routine that rapidly became familiar. They sealed the windows of their homes with gummed tape or putty and hung damp sheets in front of the windows in an attempt to filter the air. Some people covered their furniture in sheets and stuffed rags under the doors to stop the dust from seeping in. Plates, cups, and glasses were placed face down on the table until a meal was served. Housewives kept their cooking pans covered to keep dust from getting on the food. They would even mix bread dough in a drawer to try and keep the dust away. Despite all these efforts, many people went to bed during a storm to wake the next morning with dust all over the covers. Dust got into refrigerators and closets and formed ripples across the floor.

Families adopted different strategies to cope with the dust. A farmer near Griggs, Oklahoma, remembered how his wife put the meal under the tablecloth during a storm. The family would sit down to eat and, after saying grace, each member lifted up their piece of the tablecloth and ate with their head under it, out of view of the rest of the family. The editor of the *Morton County Farmer* in Kansas described how the dust got everywhere: "Is my face red—or is it black? Darn this dirt. Do I see red or do—Yes!... We can see nothing out our windows but dirt, every time our teeth come together, you feel dirt and taste it; haven't heard a thing for

•

> *"...haven't heard a thing for hours, my ears are full, can't smell, my nose is full..."*

•

hours, my ears are full, can't smell, my nose is full, can't walk, my shoes are full but not of feet."

One Kansas housewife remembered during a duster that: "All we could do was just sit in our dusty chairs and gaze at each other through the fog that filled the room and watch the fog settle slowly and silently, covering everything." Despite trying to seal up every cranny, the dust still found a way to get into the house: "Our faces were as dirty as if we had rolled in the dirt; our hair was gray and stiff and we ground dirt between our teeth."

The number of hours spent trying to keep the house clean rose dramatically during the period of the dust storms. Housewives in Oklahoma in April 1935 figured they spent 120 hours a month trying to keep their houses clean, sometimes cleaning up to four times a day. Sales of brooms, brushes, mops, and vacuum cleaners soared, and drycleaners enjoyed a boom.

To go out in a dust storm, people would cover their heads, put handkerchiefs over their faces, wear goggles to protect their eyes, and put vaseline

A solitary man clasps his hat to his head as a cloud of dust sweeps past. With low visibility and choking dust, any walk could become potentially fatal.

longer than normal. Nevertheless driving remained dangerous because of the dust drifts that formed across the highways. Roads disappeared under the dust and sand. The static electricity that accompanied dust storms short-circuited car ignitions and caused them to stall. Motorists learned to attach drag wires and chains to their cars to ground the electricity, avoid short circuits, and prevent stalling. Winds were often so strong that the blowing sand and dust stripped paint from cars and pitted windshields.

Going to school became difficult for many children. Many schools were forced to close early because of the dangers of getting children to and from school. Shoveling dust out of classrooms became a daily occurrence. However, children adapted to the conditions and still played sports and games outside in the dust storms if necessary. Baseball games were played during storms even if the ball occasionally disappeared due to bad visibility; rivalries between local towns were as sharp as ever. One of the few advantages of the storms was that the wind dislodged many Native American arrowheads: children spent hours hunting for them after storms.

In May 1932 the aviator and national hero Charles Lindbergh (see Volume 1, Chapter 4, "The Roaring Twenties") was flying from Albuquerque, New Mexico, to Kansas City, Missouri, with his wife when they flew into a dust storm. Forced to make an emergency landing on the plains in Texas, the couple spent the night in the plane before visibility improved enough for them to continue with their journey. Even the man who had single-handedly flown the Atlantic was halted, albeit temporarily, by one of the dust storms.

in their nostrils. Even after taking all these precautions, their eyes turned red and puffy, and their throats became sore. In the towns houses became unrecognizable during the dusters; during one storm a moviegoer had to crawl along the curb until he reached his neighbor's house. There were many stories of farmers getting lost on their own land when a storm hit. Sometimes they managed to find their way home by feeling along a fence wire with their hands or crawling on their hands and knees along a furrow that might lead them to the end of the field and the comparative safety of their truck. A few were not so fortunate. In western Kansas during a particularly severe storm in February 1935 one farmer drove his car off the road and started to walk the two-mile journey home. Rescuers found his body the next day—he had been suffocated by the dust as he walked. Some farmers even continued to work through the storms, using the light of their trucks to see by. Often, though, the sand and dust simply buried their farm machinery.

Travel was particularly difficult during the storms because visibility was greatly reduced. As the storms became more frequent, local people got used to driving through the dust, always with the car headlights on, though journeys took much

Thousands of sharecropping families like this one relied on the Red Cross after the drought of 1930 and 1931.

Surgeons and dentists battled to keep their instruments dust-free and sterilized. Hospital nurses in Hays, Kansas, placed wet cloths over their patients' mouths during extremely dusty periods to try to keep some of the dust out.

By late March 1935 deaths from dust pneumonia were making national and international headlines. A newspaper in Baca County, Colorado, wryly noted that by the time the deaths of six local people were reported in New York and Los Angeles, the story had been exaggerated to the extent that "…it appears that most of us were dead or dying." The paper added: "To the folks from out of the county we can truthfully say that it has been plenty bad here, but not as terrible as the eastern and far western headline writers would have you believe."

In response to the increased numbers of respiratory illnesses emergency hospitals were set up in

Colorado, Kansas, and Texas that spring. In Guymon, Oklahoma, local people converted two church basements into emergency hospitals. The Red Cross, operating out of its "dust headquarters" in Liberal, Kansas, issued an appeal for 10,000 dust masks for immediate use. By the time it left the area on May 29, 1935, the organization had given out more than 17,700 dust masks, and nurses had visited 1,631 homes to deal with dust-related illnesses.

Seeing the Funny Side

One of the most remarkable details of the Dust Bowl was the resilience and humor with which people dealt with the almost daily dust storms. Housewives joked about how they cleaned their pans by holding them up to a keyhole so that the blowing sand could scour them. Farmers said they planted their crops by throwing the seeds into the air as their fields blew past them and that birds flew backward to keep the dust out of their eyes. Hunters claimed they shot squirrels overhead as the animals burrowed

through the dust drifts for air. One man told how he put bullfrogs into a water tank, but they drowned because they had never been in water before and could not swim.

One Kansas City firm advertised small bottles of water for sale to Dust Bowl dwellers saying: "It's been a long time since you have seen any of this stuff—real genuine rain water. This specimen has been especially imported by us and bottled in our own plant." One farmer said: "I hope it'll rain before the kids grow up. They ain't never seen none." It was said that Kansans knew how to take a dust storm: "They take it on the chin, in the eyes, ears, nose, and mouth, down the neck, and in the soup."

The jokes show how the Dust Bowlers tried to not let the drought and constant storms wear them down. A pioneer spirit, sense

Murder and Suicide

The spring of 1935 was the lowest point for many Dust Bowlers, worn out by the continual dust storms, drought, and dust-related illnesses and deaths. Misery brought an increase in domestic violence, such as a woman in Morton County, Kansas, who—having cared for her father for years—suddenly killed him and then committed suicide. In another incident in the same county a drunk man shot at his his ex-wife as she sat in a cafe. She survived because the man was so drunk that the shot missed her.

of community, and hopeful optimism existed among most of the people.

DUST BOWL MIGRANTS

As farmers saw their fields turn to dust, their crops fail, and their cattle die, some gave up. More people left the region in 1935—the worst of the Dust Bowl years—than in any other year, migrating across the country to California or the industrial north in search of work. John Steinbeck's *The Grapes of Wrath* (1939) vividly portrayed the plight of the Okies, migrants from Oklahoma, as they left the plains to try for a better life in California. Such was the book's impact that many people inextricably linked the Dust Bowl with the migration.

While some Dust Bowlers did migrate, the majority remained in the region. The migrants who left in their thousands for the West usually came from the cotton pickers and sharecroppers of Arkansas and southern Oklahoma.

•

"I hope it'll rain before the kids grow up. They ain't never seen none."

•

In 1930 the population of the Oklahoma panhandle stood at 30,960. Ten years later it was 22,198, a fall of 8,762. In 1936, in seven counties in southeastern Colorado only 2,078 of 6,411 homes remained occupied.

DUST BOWL ECONOMY

Despite the fact that so much of the land was turning to dust, land values held up better in the Dust Bowl than in less arid areas. The economy of the Dust Bowl—with the exception of farming— remained little worse than that of

any other region. Certain parts of the Great Plains, particularly early in the Depression, experienced their greatest boom. Modernization by the railroad, oil, and gas industries provided money and employment. The dust storms actually helped the transition from an agricultural to a industrial economy. From 1929 to 1931 the Texas and Oklahoma panhandles were among the most prosperous areas in the nation. Towns undertook extensive building and development—paving streets, expanding water systems, improving sewers, starting highways and airports, and building facilities such as golf courses and swimming pools. Smaller towns got electricity and telephone lines for the first time. As the oil and gas business boomed in 1936, so many people moved into Sunray, Texas, that

A service station in Dalhart, Texas, is an indicator of the thriving oil and gas industries.

People sing together in Pie Town, New Mexico, a community settled by migrant Dust Bowl farmers from Oklahoma and Texas.

they caused a housing shortage and made it necessary to expand the railroad.

Most banks stayed open in the Dust Bowl area during the Depression. Newspapers, post offices, and businesses largely survived the decade unscathed. Small towns had already suffered as people drove to larger towns to do business, and small farms had become unprofitable: The dust storms speed up both processes. Farming families learned to survive on very little, much as the homesteaders had done when they first arrived in the area.

Farmers returned to subsistence farming, growing food for their families. Some families had wheat for three meals a day: Their diet consisted of cereals, macaroni, cookies, and bread. One family lived on water gravy, bread, and rabbit meat; jack rabbits provided many families with their only source of meat. Fortunate families cultivated a vegetable and fruit garden; but as Dust Bowl conditions intensified, gardens became difficult to maintain, and instead they resorted to bottled and preserved fruit and vegetables.

COMMUNITY AND RELIGION

Tough as life was in the Dust Bowl, many people stayed on, knowing that life could be equally hard elsewhere. At home there were friends, a community spirit, a sense of tradition and history, and for some, the church to sustain them through the hardest times. During the 1930s church attendance rose across the Dust Bowl region, although some people stopped going to church

because they could no longer afford proper Sunday clothing.

One farmer recalled his Baptist preacher in Hooker, Oklahoma, telling the congregation that "the Lord had put them there for a reason, and it was their obligation to remain." Different branches of the Christian church, such as the Quakers and Methodists, gained new members during the thirties, and new churches were built to house growing congregations. In Wilburton, Kansas, the local Methodist congregation raised funds to pay the pastor to switch from part-time to full-time duties. With the arrival of a permanent pastor church membership soared by over 100 percent. Fundamentalist sects, meanwhile, interpreted

One of the few remaining occupied farms in Coldwater District, north of Dalhart, Texas, in 1938. Most of the other Dust Bowl farms in the district had been abandoned.

Countering Negative Publicity

The editor of the Dalhart *Texan*, John L. McCarty, organized the "Last Man's Club" in April 1935. Membership was open only to those who pledged to be the last man to leave the Dust Bowl. About a hundred men joined. McCarty was eager to promote a sense of pride in the region and to counter the negative publicity he felt the national media gave the Dust Bowl. In "A Tribute to Our Sandstorms," an article he wrote after watching the dramatic beauty of an approaching storm—the sunlight revealed its deep shades of purple, blue, and dark green—McCarty sang the praises of the region. McCarty and other local journalists particularly objected to articles like Walter Davenport's "Land Where Our Children Die," published in *Collier's* on September 18, 1937, and the film, *The Plow That Broke the Plains*, made on behalf of the Resettlement Administration in 1936. They argued that such articles and movies promoted an image of the Dust Bowl populated by incompetent farmers and desperate people.

It was a national journalist who coined the phrase "Dust Bowl." After the roller of April 14, 1935, an Associated Press reporter, Robert Geiger, wrote "Three little words—achingly familiar on a Western farmer's tongue—rule life today in the dust bowl of the continent... If it rains." The Washington *Evening Star* printed Geiger's article, and the name "Dust Bowl" caught on immediately across the nation.

A pioneer woman of the Oklahoma panhandle Dust Bowl in 1936. Although many people did abandon the region, others resolved to stay.

the storms as a sign that the end of the world was imminent.

The sense of community and neighborhood was further fostered by many incidents of help and rescue. During storms people got lost on the roads and in the fields, and friends and neighbors would search for them until they were found. Countless stories exist, such as that of a seven-year-old boy caught in a storm in Kansas and found the next day smothered to death by dust. A nine-year-old boy stranded in the same storm was luckier: Rescuers found him alive but tangled in barbed wire. The resilient spirit was mostly overlooked by the people elsewhere who asked why more Dust Bowlers did not leave the region.

Leveling fields as part of a project to prevent wind erosion near Liberal, Kansas, 1936.

OPTIMISM

The phrase "if it rains" became a byword for the whole Dust Bowl region, capturing the optimistic hope that kept many people living on amid drought and dust. One resident of Baca County, Colorado, wrote: "With real pioneer courage we are doing our best to make the most of a bad condition.... We feel toward our country as parents toward a wayward child. We love it in spite of the wind and drought. Only the faint-hearted will move away. The pioneers will stay, plant trees, and trust in God." Ultimately, the people of the Dust Bowl stayed because they believed in the region's positive future. Just as the terrible droughts at the end of the 19th century had eventually ended for a previous generation of farmers, so the current generation believed that it would eventually rain, and the area would prosper once more.

3. FEDERAL AID FOR FARMERS

Once the relief organizations of Roosevelt's administration started to address the farmers' plight, their livestock, and the soil degradation, it did not make financial sense to move away. One farmer near Boise City, Oklahoma, said: "If I leave, I can't get wheat and corn payments on relief and that's all that keeps me alive." Many farmers stayed in the region as a result of subsidies, loans, and support from the Federal Emergency Relief Administration (FERA), Agricultural Adjustment Administration (AAA), and Farm Credit Administration, which allowed farmers to buy fuel, animal feed, seeds, food, and clothing. Other small farmers were bought out as the government bought up land.

SOIL CONSERVATION SERVICE

Although the dust storms continued until 1939, effective measures to halt wind erosion had begun much earlier. The storms forced farmers to reconsider their land-management techniques and address the need for soil conservation. In 1935 the Soil Conservation Service (SCS) began to address the problem of turning the Dust Bowl back to grassland. The government compulsorily purchased thousands of acres of land and required some farmers to move so that their land could be returned to grasslands. Working alongside the SCS, the farmers made great progress in reducing erosion across the Dust Bowl.

As early as August 1933 farmers began using new methods to aid conservation. Terracing and contour plowing, in which furrows followed the shape of the land rather than running in straight lines, helped prevent soil blowing away. FERA gave the state of Kansas $250,000 in spring 1935 to carry out emergency listing, a form of plowing in which furrows were protected on either side by ridges of earth, again greatly reducing wind erosion. Farmers were paid 10 cents an acre to list any land susceptible to blowing.

By the end of 1935 the SCS had 47 projects underway covering 40 million acres, with another 8 million acres and 94 projects under supervision. An example of a successful SCS project was the transformation of Dalhart, Texas, one of the worst affected areas of the Dust Bowl. Continuous blowing had reduced a large area to a desert; rippled sand dunes like something from the seaside stood 30 feet high. Within the space of 15 months the initiatives launched by the SCS had transformed the area into a green carpet capable of again producing crops.

END OF THE EXODUS

The work of the SCS and the federal aid money finally halted the exodus of farmers from the

Positive Results

The results of conservation methods of farming were quick to show. The rains of May 1935 soaked into the earth, and ground cover started to regrow. By 1936 wind erosion had been cut by half. By December 1937 farmers had reduced the amount of seriously eroded land by 65 to 70 percent over the previous year. Finally the summer rains of 1938 helped reduce the Dust Bowl to its smallest size since 1932.

Marion Olsen, a Farm Security Administration "graduate," with his daughter at home in Utah in 1940. Olsen borrowed $12,000 from the FSA and paid it back when the fortunes of his farm improved.

Dust Bowl. In some areas the population even grew. In a 27-county area of southwestern Kansas the number of farmers actually increased from 22,369 to 23,916 between 1930 and 1935. With federal aid farmers were also able to increase the total acreage of their farms during the same period—from 73.4 percent to 78.4 percent of the Kansan Dust Bowl area—working on the principle that a greater amount of land would produce a higher crop yield. The fact remained that even with this increased land, farmers in 1935 harvested the equivalent of less than half of the cereal crop of 1930.

The work of the SCS and the crucial importance of sustainable farming techniques helped arrest the dust damage of the 1930s. When the rains started to fall again at the end of the decade, the farmers soon found that their harvests increased. In the Texas panhandle the 1939 harvest was more than six times greater than that of 1935.

4. WORLD WAR II AND BEYOND

The arrival of the rains was followed by the outbreak of World War II in Europe in 1939. The conflict fueled demand for U.S. wheat, cotton, and beef. Prices rose so high that farmers forgot the traumas of the previous decade. Many started to abandon sustainable farming in an effort to plant as much as possible. The 1950s brought new dust storms; and although conditions never reached the extremes of the 1930s, it was a salutory lesson in farming management.

4

CALIFORNIA IN THE 1930s

The image of California as the land of plenty attracted migrants from poorer states to go and settle there. Some were welcomed as a source of cheap labor. Others, particularly the Okies, were resented and badly treated.

In the mid-1930s more than a million of the migrants who left the Dust Bowl headed for California. A folk song, "Why We Come to California," captures some of their expectations.

Dust Bowl refugees from Oklahoma newly arrived in San Fernando, California, June 1935.

California, California,
Here I come too.
With a coffee pot and skillet,
And I'm coming to you.
Nothing's left in Oklahoma,
For us to eat or do.
And if apples, nuts, and oranges,
And Santy Claus is real,
Come on to California,
Eat and eat 'til you're full.

Interstate migration to California was hardly new. People had headed west first for the Gold Rush in 1849, then for booms in the 1880s and 1920s. The latter decade saw a rise of 60 percent in California's population, from 3,426,861 to 5,677,251. Of the 2.25 million new arrivals, 1.8 million were interstate migrants:

Grapes grown in Kern County, California, 1936. Images like this helped build a picture of California as the land of plenty.

The rest came from Mexico, Asia, and Europe. Some Californians complained about the number of new arrivals. The economy was booming, however, and most arrivals found work. Even in the worst years of the Depression, between 1930 and 1932, the average Californian's income was $635, compared to $298 in Texas. The influx of outsiders, however, overwhelmed local and state resources. Californians reacted with racist and nativist attitudes, and a fear of immigrant labor. Discrimination against the outsiders only ended when

1. THE DUST BOWL MIGRANTS

The California migration that took place in the 1930s was very different from that of the 1920s. It

Route 66

Throughout the 1920s open-top touring cars, or "flivvers," laden down with people and possessions, arrived in California via Route 66, also known as Highway 66. All along the road an industry grew up dedicated to serving travelers' needs. Auto-camps, forerunners of the motel, gas stations, diners, and road houses—which offered both legal and illegal services—sprang up. John Steinbeck wrote about the road's importance as an artery for the Okies.

also differed from that which came later, in the 1940s, when World War II required thousands of workers for shipyards, munitions factories, and agriculture.

Most of the more than 300,000 interstate migrants who arrived in California between 1930 and 1934 were the displaced and dispossessed. They were dubbed "Dust Bowl migrants" by journalists who associated the large numbers of automobiles heading west on Route 66 with the drought conditions of the Dust Bowl. Although their exodus reached its peak in 1935, coinciding with the worst dust storms, the migrants in fact came from a variety of origins.

THE OKIES

The majority of migrants who flooded into California actually came from Arkansas, Missouri, Oklahoma, and Texas, only the last two of which lay even partly in the Dust Bowl. They were largely tenant farmers and share-croppers who worked the cotton fields. They were escaping the effects of drought and the failure

of the cotton crop. More significantly their labor had been increasingly replaced by tractors and other machines. Nicknamed the "Okies," these predominantly white Protestant farmers struggled to make a new life in the agricultural heartland of California. More than any other migrant group, they faced hostility from resident Californians, which flared into anti-Okie hysteria in 1938.

ON THE ROAD

One of the lasting images of the 1930s Dust Bowl migration is a jalopy with a family and all its possessions precariously loaded on board. The 1,200-mile (1,931-km) journey from Oklahoma to California was made possible by the car. In 1931 a total of 876,194 cars entered the state. Some migrants left most of their possessions behind, either because they never intended to stay in California or as a precaution in case things did not work out. The cotton pickers, for example, followed a "cotton loop" through Texas, Arizona, California, and

A Missouri family on the roadside in Tracy, California, 1937. They are broke and experiencing car trouble.

then home, matching their arrival in each place with the picking season. Lumber workers had their own annual circuit.

While some migrants rode the trains and buses, hopped freight trains, or hitched lifts, the majority traveled by car. A space in a California-bound car cost $10, but most migrants had their own vehicle. In a reliable auto the journey could be done in as little as three days.

For many it was an exciting experience. Old cars broke down, however, and travelers ran out of money for food or gas. Some would stop in Arizona and pick

cotton to earn enough money to continue their journey; some of them never made it to California. Many could not afford the auto-camps that had been built to service migrants in the twenties. Instead, they pulled off the

California Movies

For many Americans their only knowledge of California before they moved there came through the movies. Often the California shown on film was a land of opportunity and bounty, as W. C. Fields' 1934 comedy *It's a Gift* demonstrates. Fields plays an incompetent storekeeper from New Jersey who buys an orange grove in southern California. He and his family move to California, discover their land to be worthless, and are seemingly destined to join California's poor. At the last minute a property developer buys the grove for a huge sum, and the family ends up living in luxury. Hollywood movies and magazines describing film stars' lives also helped create an image of California few would ever see.

In It's a Gift *W. C. Fields (right) plays a storekeeper who buys a useless plot of land in California.*

The Promised Land

The families who moved west during the 1930s had heard about southern California's legendary climate, where the sun shone continually, and ripe oranges could be picked straight from the tree. The variety of agricultural crops grown—from grapes and peas to cotton—commanded deep reverence from the Okies.

Many myths had grown up about California as the promised land and about how easy life was there. The idea of California as the land of plenty and opportunity can be traced back to the arrival of early settlers during the 19th century.

The history of American migration has always been westward. Families moved because they wanted to make a fresh start. California, geographically the United States' final frontier, also acquired a symbolic status as a kind of promised land to reach for which any sacrifice or transgression was justified.

The geographical and symbolic status of California came together in the famed story of the Donner-Reed party, pioneers who traveled from Illinois to California in 1846. Caught in a snowstorm in the California Sierras, members of the party froze to death. In order to stay alive, their companions ate the flesh of the dead. The survivors went on to settle in California. The story suggests that the sacrifice of the dead and the cannibalism of the living somehow indicated the great value of the final prize, California.

California's symbolic status was further complicated by the discovery of gold near Sacramento in 1848. The image of the state was transformed from a place where enterprise and hard work would be rewarded to a paradise where fortunes might be made without extreme effort.

After the start of the Gold Rush in 1849, and California's statehood in 1850, thousands flocked to the state and discovered it still had more to offer. Dubbed "the golden state" for the gold in the Sierra Nevada, the nickname also applied to the weather. Huge tracts of arable land added to its mythical image as a land of milk and honey. The nationwide promotion of southern California as a sun-drenched paradise started in the 1880s; one advertisement read, "In California…you live life, elsewhere you merely spend it."

There is a reverse side to the promised land, as modern-day writers such as Sacramento-native Joan Didion have pointed out. California is also the last-chance saloon, the final frontier. America literally runs out of land at the Pacific Ocean. For those who fail to discover their promised land there, there is nowhere else to go.

Gold diggers crowd the western shore of the Sacramento River during the 1849 California Gold Rush in this contemporary lithograph.

A combine harvester in a wheat field in the San Joaquin Valley, 1938. Machinery often took work from farm laborers.

highway at the end of a day's driving and camped by the road. As trucks thundered past, families would make campfires and cook what provisions they had. The next day they would continue along Route 66, passing through Mississippi, Oklahoma, Texas, New Mexico, Arizona, and Nevada, to California.

When the Okies reached California, two options presented themselves at the Barstow exit. They could stay on the highway all the way to Los Angeles, or they could leave the road and journey north, following the still partially unpaved roads over the Tehachapi Mountains to the San Joaquin Valley. The splitting of the road neatly symbolized the very different fates of those who chose the city and those who chose the countryside.

2. RURAL CALIFORNIA

Three fertile inland valleys dominated and still dominate California's agriculture: the great Central Valley stretches from Chico in the north to Bakersfield in the south and splits into the Sacramento and San Joaquin valleys. The Sacramento Valley is humid and can sustain crops naturally, while the San Joaquin Valley needs intensive irrigation. Further south the Imperial Valley has been reclaimed from desert and requires constant watering.

The three valleys, along with smaller agricultural areas, have produced a variety of crops since the wheat bonanzas of the 1870s. Fruit cultivation, followed by sugar beets, and then cotton in the 1920s produced healthy profits. By 1930 more than 180 different crops grew in California over the whole year. Some small farms still existed, but they could not compete financially with the large-scale corporate farms that had come to dominate the state's agriculture.

MIGRATORY WORKFORCE

The ranch owners who controlled the central valleys had established a system of farming that relied on the cheapest possible workforce. They argued that cheap labor helped compensate for other fluctuating costs caused by good or bad harvests. Cotton and fruit growing required short, intense

In a large-scale operation in the Imperial Valley in 1939 Mexican and white gang labor pulls, cleans, ties, and crates carrots for the eastern market. Working for 11 cents per crate of 48 bunches, most workers made barely $1 per day.

Mexican laborers off to work in the melon fields of California's Imperial Valley, June 1935.

periods of work during harvest times and then nothing for months. Rather than hire laborers to work the whole year, ranchers employed workers to pick the crop as quickly as possible and then leave. Between 1870 and 1930 a system of migratory labor had evolved that relied almost exclusively on Chinese, Japanese, Hindu, Filipino, and Mexican workers. Such overseas workers, who enjoyed few rights and had no organized labor unions, were easy to exploit.

Mexican Seasonal Workers

The Mexicans were the most successful ethnic migrant workers. Some 150,000 Mexicans and Mexican Americans worked in the Californian fields prior to 1930. They were skillful, working efficiently and speedily; when the picking season ended, they returned to Mexico or traveled to the urban centers of Fresno, Bakers-field, and Los Angeles, where they went on relief.

The growers benefited from huge profits and low labor costs. With the start of the Depression, however, California's cities could no longer afford to subsidize the harvest-relief cycles. In 1930 cities like Los Angeles began a program of voluntary repatriation for Mexicans and Mexican Americans to Mexico City. Relief authorities paid the $14.70 bus fare to Mexico City. Many Mexicans were eager to try their luck back in Mexico on the strength of rumors of land reform. Between February 1931 and early 1933 up to 75,000 Mexicans took up the offer. Others, including American citizens, were expelled by force. By 1937 about 150,000 Mexicans had left California; few newcomers were entering the United States because of the Depression (see Volume 5, Chapter 2, "Equality for Some").

Labor Shortage

Although many Mexicans and Mexican Americans remained in California, ranch owners were concerned about labor. By mid-1933 both labor and production shortages were occurring. They liked to have more workers available than there were jobs, so that competition would keep wages down. But from a peak of 186 workers for every 100 agricultural jobs in early 1933 the number had fallen to 142 by 1934. Meanwhile, Mexican farm workers were becoming increasingly unionized. They struck for better working conditions and pay in 1933 and 1934.

OKIES IN THE VALLEYS

It was into this situation that the new stream of Okies came. Whole families of Okies arrived in the California valleys to meet up with their family and friends, many of whom had arrived there in the

Factories-in-the-Field

Unlike other farming states across the nation, California does not have a history of significant small tenant farming. The 160-acre farm on which homesteading was founded throughout the West never existed in California. Most farms were huge, earning them the title "factories-in-the-field." When California was still part of Mexican territory, it was divided into huge estates. Following the Mexican War of 1848, America gained the territory, inheriting the estates intact. The model for the agricultural regions became huge ranches that were farmed intensively.

1920s. Almost two-thirds of the migrants to the Salinas Valley had relatives already there, as did 47 percent of the newcomers to the Sacramento Valley. It was a similar story in Kern County and across most of the San Joaquin Valley, the largest and most productive of all California's agricultural areas. Between 1935 and 1940 more than 70,000 Okies put down roots in the San Joaquin Valley, particularly in Kern County, because its cotton and oil economy most closely resembled those of Texas and Oklahoma to which they were accustomed.

The fertile San Joaquin Valley produced three to four times as much cotton as the cotton-producing areas of Oklahoma. California's farmers had expanded

A sign advertises for cotton pickers in the southern San Joaquin Valley in 1936. At first the Okies provided a welcome source of labor.

Rural Population Boom

The Okie migration reversed the trend in which cities were the fastest growing population centers. During the twenties the cities—particularly Los Angeles—had expanded more rapidly than anywhere else. Between 1935 and 1940 the San Joaquin Valley—except Fresno County—grew faster than Los Angeles. During the thirties 180,000 Okie migrants took up residence in the countryside, most of them in the San Joaquin Valley. Kern County's population increased by 63.6 percent in the second half of the decade.

their cotton acreage substantially during the early part of the decade. In 1932 they farmed 123,000 acres; by 1936 this had risen to 620,000 acres. Because cotton pickers were in short supply, wages rose from 45 cents per 100 pounds of picked cotton in 1932 to $1 in 1936. Many Okies were expert cotton pickers, and they wanted to capitalize on the high wages.

At first the ranchers welcomed the new labor force. However, as they arrived in the valleys, the Okies were unwittingly upsetting the social and political structure that had been in place for at least 60 years. The ranch owners relied on migratory, single, male workers to pick their crops. The Okies, by contrast, usually arrived as family units. Of the single men and women who migrated to California, many tried their luck in the cities rather than the fields.

The Okies who arrived in the rural areas stood out for a number of reasons. First, they were not spread evenly across the state. Since most of them wanted to work on the cotton farms, or less realistically to buy their own farm,

they were concentrated mainly in the cotton-growing regions. Second, they did not arrive in consistent numbers. Nearly half of the decade's migrants arrived in a three-year period between 1935 and 1937. Third, most of the Okies planned to stay permanently in California. Unlike the Mexican migrant workers, they did not leave after the harvest. Most families registered in order to claim relief, which they could initially do after living in the state for a year. Once they had registered as residents, they were also entitled to vote in California elections. This would have profound political consequences as the decade went on.

FINDING WORK

Two problems faced the Okies as they descended from the Tehachapi Pass: getting work and finding somewhere to sleep. Some farmers did manage to fulfill their dreams and buy a few acres for their own farms, but land costs in the San Joaquin Valley were five to ten times those in Oklahoma, at about $200 an acre. During the twenties 20 percent of California's farms had been farmed by tenants, but the Depression led to foreclosures and the consolidation of smaller farms. By the thirties renting land was difficult.

By 1940 only 2 percent of the recent migrants owned, leased, or managed farms, compared with 10 percent of earlier settlers. A few of the new arrivals found employment in nonagricultural sectors like oil and construction. By 1940, 29 percent of all construction workers in the San Joaquin Valley were Dust Bowl migrants.

Some families set up businesses, catering to the needs of the new arrivals; grocery stands, lunch counters, and repair services opened and closed with regularity. Most migrants, however, sought work picking cotton or fruit on one of the huge ranches.

Cotton Picking

Most families timed their arrival to coincide with the start of the cotton-picking season, which lasted two months into December. A skilled picker could pick as much as 300 to 400 pounds of cotton a day and earn between $3 and $4. Since the wage was twice that in Oklahoma and the cotton was easier to pick, skilled pickers felt they had arrived in the land of plenty. Over a season they could earn a sizable amount of money. Many were tempted to stay on and try their hand at other crops.

From December to March there was little harvesting work,

Loading cotton in the San Joaquin Valley. The need for cotton pickers was great, and the Okies were experienced at the work.

however, and the migrants had to rely on whatever they had been able to save. Neither did cotton pickers necessarily make good fruit pickers, as the manager of the San Joaquin Valley Agricultural Labor Bureau explained: "These people know cotton but they cannot make a year-round living in cotton alone…. They can squat and sort, but they cannot squat and walk, like a Mexican; hence they are not good in asparagus. They do not know how to handle fruit as yet— but they will learn."

OKIES IN THE CITIES

Less than a quarter of all interstate migrants moved to California's urban centers. Census

figures put the number of Oklahomans, Texans, Arkansans, and Missourians who arrived in Los Angeles in the second half of the 1930s at nearly 100,000. The San Francisco Bay area and San Diego were much less popular: Between them they attracted only one-quarter of the urban arrivals.

Los Angeles

The Los Angeles area absorbed more new arrivals than any other urban area. Migrants were often initially overwhelmed by the size of the place. None had ever been in such a big city, which sprawled over 450 square miles (1,165 sq km). One migrant from Guymon, Oklahoma (population: 3,000),

Two migrant workers pass an ironic billboard as they head for Los Angeles in the hope of finding work in March 1937.

described the move to an area of 2.3 million inhabitants as "going into an entirely different world…. It seemed like you could drive forever and never get out of a town." The famous folk musician Woody Guthrie (1912–1967) was no less intimidated by the city: "Los Angeles is too big for me. I'm too little for Los Angeles."

Los Angeles was not an easy place to settle, but many chose the city because they had family and friends who were already living there. Knowing somebody could help with finding a job and a place to live. Three-quarters of the 800 men who built cars for Southern Pacific Railroad were from the Okie region: "Most of them all relatives…uncles, fathers, sons… everybody knew everybody," recalled one migrant.

Finding Work

Finding work in the cities was hard but not impossible for white migrants who possessed any type of skills. Black or Hispanic workers found it far more impossible to find jobs. Professional and white-collar workers had the least difficulty in finding

•

"Los Angeles is too big for me. I'm too little for Los Angeles."

•

work, while experienced blue-collar workers could usually get something. Two rapidly expanding industries in southern California were in aircraft and autos, and experienced workers were in demand. Construction and oil jobs—the two most common industries in Oklahoma and Texas—were harder to secure because both were hit by the Depression. Those migrants with no skill base—often those who had come from the farms—did casual jobs, working on a day-to-day basis on construction sites, digging ditches, clearing fields, and even picking fruit in the metropolitan area's numerous citrus groves.

FINDING ACCOMMODATION

Rural or urban, most migrant families were short of money when they first arrived in California, having spent most, if not all, of their savings on getting there. They could not pay for a motel or rent a place to live right away. Instead, they pitched their tents in the irrigation ditches and empty fields near the large ranches or moved into private trailer camps. A fortunate few who found work immediately lived in grower-maintained living quarters, which, despite their squalid state, provided some shelter from the winter. For those forced to camp, conditions were worse than those they had left behind. The sudden arrival of 300,000 migrants in a relatively small area in a short time created a housing and health

Los Angeles in the 1930s

Los Angeles was still recovering from the Depression and a peak of 30 percent unemployment in early 1933 when the first Okie migrants arrived. The Los Angeles area absorbed more arrivals than any other conurbation. Unemployment and homelessness were a feature of Los Angeles life throughout the decade, and relief expenditure was huge. During the summer of 1935, 350,000 residents (15 percent of the population) relied on public assistance.

An 18-year-old mother from Oklahoma with her child, both California migrants, outside their primitive tent home.

disaster. The California State Commission of Immigration and Housing had been created in 1921 to deal with just this sort of problem. Political wranglings, however, left the commission by the 1930s with only a skeleton staff that was unable to help the migrants in any meaningful way.

OKIE CHILDREN

Inadequate housing had a harmful effect on the health of the Okie children. They lived on a diet of beans and fried dough, with virtually no milk or fresh fruit and vegetables. Between July 1936 and June 1937 a survey of 1,000 migrant children in the San Joaquin Valley found that 831 were suffering from a total of 1,369 illnesses, mostly caused by malnutrition and bad hygiene.

Vaccinating children for smallpox and typhoid fever in a squatter camp in Visalia, California, 1939. White migrants generally enjoyed far better facilities than black, Hispanic, or Asian workers.

Many of the children had to work with their parents to bring in enough money to feed the family. Schooling was intermittent at best; in the Bakersfield area 48.6 percent of all school-age children transferred schools at least once in 1935 as their families moved around in search of work. When

the Okie children did go to school—hungry, poorly dressed, and barefoot—they were often picked on by the local children.

OKIE PARENTS

The same fate often met the Okie parents. Their poverty, squalid housing, dirty and unkempt appearance, and accents all distinguished them from local people. Their religious practices—which included snake handling, speaking in tongues, and rolling on the ground—further marked them out. As the decade went on, they found themselves increasingly targeted for discrimination. This was the beginning of anti-Okie resentment.

The chief reason for resident Californians turning against the latest arrivals was economic. The ranch owners who had welcomed the Okies' labor nevertheless resented their refusal to continue

Okie Accommodations

The migrants lived in four types of settlement: private labor camps, auto and trailer camps, shacktowns, and the ditch-bank and roadside squatter camps. None of them was meant for long-term stays since they did not have adequate sanitation and washing facilities.

The private labor camps consisted of one-room frame cabins, often in a dilapidated state, tents, or farm buildings such as chickensheds and barns, which were converted into dormitories. The camps were unregulated and uninspected, and the migrants were at the mercy of the unscrupulous owners, who usually did nothing to improve the buildings.

Above: Dorothea Lange took this picture of a migrant workers camp in California's Imperial Valley in 1937. The most desperate families did not even have the luxury of a tent—they slept in their cars.

The auto and trailer camps were located on roadsides and offered better accommodations than the labor camps, but they became so overcrowded that they were unsanitary and a health threat.

In the shacktowns, known as Little Oklahomas or Hoovervilles, migrants erected their own cabins, tents, or other housing on land that had been subdivided by local farmers. In one Little Oklahoma outside Modesto the land was subdivided in 1935, with a lot costing $125. Families put down $10 and then paid $5 a month. By 1938 more than 200 families—approximately 1,000 people—lived there. Eventually these families made the transition from a haphazard collection of tents, trailers, packing boxes, cardboard, tarpaper, and gunny sacks for housing to whitewashed frame houses, but it took years to accomplish. One Oklahoman said proudly: "The houses have been

Photographed in Visalia, California, in 1939 this squatter camp is made up of disused refrigerator boxcars lined up beside an irrigation ditch. The community even had its own doctor's office, again based in a boxcar.

built jist a piece at a time.... If a man saves any money he adds a little more on." In the meantime, the shacktowns were full of garbage, stank of human waste, and were buzzing with flies, much to the horror of many Californians, who resented their squalid appearance on the edge of their towns.

The shacktowns, labor camps, and auto camps were infinitely better than the ditch-bank dwellings—often the first homes for the newly arrived Okies. As the migration reached its peak in 1936 and 1937, more ditch-bank settlements were started, and the existing ones grew bigger. When the Okies put up their tents in the ditches, they assumed it would be for a short time. For many, however, the ditches became home, but without any sanitation, water, or basic facilities of any kind. The lack of proper sanitation and water led to disease. Typhoid, smallpox, tuberculosis, malaria, and pneumonia were all present in the camps. As early as 1934 local health officials had recognized the

A migrant winter camp on the outskirts of Sacramento is home to 80 migrant families. They built their own shacks and paid $1.25 per month in ground rent, which included water.

potential health hazard of the settlements and ordered the migrants to move on and the camps to be burned. Kern County led the way in destroying the camps, but it did not solve the problem. The evicted Okies, unable to afford anything else, moved down the road and set up another camp.

with the Mexican migratory work pattern of moving on when a job was finished. For the Okies themselves, remaining in one place meant long periods without work. Not even the fertile San Joaquin Valley, where potatoes, grapes, and cotton matured at different times, could offer year-round work.

Families nevertheless needed to keep earning. Husbands would look for manual labor on construction sites or in factories. However, since they could realistically travel no further than 20 to 30 miles (32 to 48 km) from their home base, jobs were not easy to find. During the peak season women were employed in the canneries.

CLAIMING RELIEF

Attempts to find work were often unfruitful. In the long periods of unemployment the Okies fell back on claiming relief. By June 1934, 1,225,000 Californians out of a population of six million depended on public aid. In Los Angeles

Crowds of migrant workers wait for relief checks in Calipatria, Imperial Valley, 1937.

County alone over 465,000 people were claiming relief. With only 4.7 percent of America's population, California had 14 percent of all its transients.

The southern counties of the San Joaquin Valley, particularly Kern County, had absorbed 37 percent of the migrants who arrived between 1935 and 1939. Kings, Tulare, Fresno, and Madera counties were swamped by new arrivals. Between 1937 and 1939 the number of people receiving state unemployment relief in Kern County increased from 8,975 to 45,391. To pay for the extra relief, local taxes doubled between 1935 and 1940. During the same period school enrolment in the county increased by 300 percent, creating more expense. In adjacent Los Angeles County there was an 80 percent increase in relief and 55 percent in taxes. Resentment started to grow among local residents, who faced higher bills.

3. INCREASING RESENTMENT

Until 1938 the rest of California, let alone the rest of the country,

remained unaware of the growing migrant problem in Kern and the other southern San Joaquin Valley counties. Before 1938 most Californians tended to view Depression arrivals not as migrants but as transients; they were used to influxes of men seeking work. Even before 1931 an estimated 10,000 transient men and boys arrived in Los Angeles County each month. The assumption was that they would leave when the Depression ended.

In August 1935, however, the federal government stopped its aid to transients. Californians started to worry that every transient in the country would make for the golden state and then claim state benefits. In an attempt to dissuade any prospective migrants, the state implemented draconian measures.

In Los Angeles County police operated a "bum blockade" (see box, page 78), treating transients as criminals by booking and fingerprinting them. Other forces, such as the Fresno police, operated a shelter at the city limits to keep transients out of town. For the next two years the migrant issue

The Los Angeles police border patrol prevents a group of men from crossing the bridge from Arizona into California, 1936. The so-called "bum blockade" to stop migrants entering California was later ruled unconstitutional.

simmered, although the worst-affected agricultural areas were unable to sustain interest in the problem across the rest of the state, far less beyond California's state lines.

FEDERAL AID FOR OKIES

Despite the indifference of the rest of the state and country to the growing Okie problem, some individuals took their plight seriously and carried sufficient influence among the New Dealers in Washington, D.C., to be able to instigate programs to help them. In 1935 the Resettlement Administration (RA) came into being. One of its more controversial aims was to place more tenant farmers on their own properties. The Farm Security Administration (FSA) replaced the RA in 1937 and lasted until 1942. Gradually some improvements came in migrant housing and health. Generally, however, the federal response was inadequate.

Federal Camps

Paul Taylor, economics professor at the University of California at Berkeley, was instrumental in bringing the plight of the migrants to a wider audience. He set in motion a process that resulted in the construction of federal housing camps at Marysville, Tuba County, and Arvin, in Kern County (see box, page 76). An expert on the economic and social crisis created by the Dust Bowl migration, Taylor documented the disintegration and degradation of migrant life in facts and figures. His second wife, the photographer Dorothea Lange, captured images of the Okies such as *Migrant Mother*, which became the defining picture of the crisis. Their collaborative book, *American Exodus* (1939), stands alongside John Steinbeck's *The Grapes of Wrath* as one of the key works of the Depression.

4. CHANGING POLITICAL SCENE

Ranch owners objected to the federal camps because they feared the Okies were being encouraged to be too independent and might

Migrant or Resident?

In 1937 Kern County's board of supervisors sent President Roosevelt a telegram asking for federal aid, arguing that since the migrants were not Californians, the problem of how to pay for them was a federal one. This raised an important question: When did a migrant stop being a migrant and become a resident? For many Okies California was their new home. For the Californians, however, the Okies' presence had become undesirable. By 1938 the call was for the Okies to be sent back to their states of origin.

Federal Camps

Children singing in Sunday School in Marysville Camp, 1938. Although many are wearing overalls, they look clean and healthy. Four ministers took turns holding services in the camp.

The first two federal migrant camps, Marysville Camp and Arvin Camp, were in stark contrast to the private labor camps and squalid ditch-bank settlements where the migrants had been living. Work started on Marysville Camp in July 1935, and the construction of the Arvin Camp followed shortly afterward.

Paul Taylor, the driving force behind the camps, planned to build 25 camps across the western United States; by 1939 the Farm Security Administration was running 10 camps in California alone. Each of these camps had a clinic and nurse, a recreation hall, a camp school or busing to local schools, a library, an amphitheater for meetings and movies, and often a baseball diamond.

In Marysville Camp 230 families lived in one-room frame cabins and shared a communal cooking shed and a sanitary building that contained

A small library in the Arvin Camp, run by a Works Progress Administration librarian. Libraries were an important aspect of the recreation and education program instituted in all the federal migrant camps.

A Saturday night dance at the Tulare migrant camp, Visalia, in 1940. So popular were the dance evenings that hundreds of people from outside the camp also attended them.

showers, toilets, and laundry tubs. There was also a first-aid dispensary and a children's nursery. The Arvin Camp, in contrast, consisted of more substantial houses with plumbing and electricity that could be rented for $8.20 a month, including utilities. By 1940 there were more than 500 houses available to rent at the camp.

The Arvin Camp—the model for Steinbeck's Weedpatch Camp in *The Grapes of Wrath*—was run by Thomas Collins, to whom Steinbeck dedicated his book, and provided the strongest contrast with any of the private facilities. The camp was self-governing and had its own rules and regulations. A strong sense of community was fostered by musical evenings, games, sports, and regular dances. Residents would gather around the campfire in the evenings and sing folk songs. As a result, Bakersfield, the nearest town, became one of the nation's country-and-western centers.

The camps helped the migrants regain their sense of dignity and independence; they were clean, well fed, and smartly dressed for the first time since their arrival in California. People were vaccinated against smallpox and other diseases, and women were introduced to the concept of family planning; previously it had not been uncommon for migratory mothers to have a child every year from their teens into their thirties.

Some 45,000 migrants (one-fifth of the total) lived in federal camps or rented federal housing. The camps were predominantly white, however. For Mexican, Chinese, Japanese, Filipino, and black workers such facilities were rare or nonexistent.

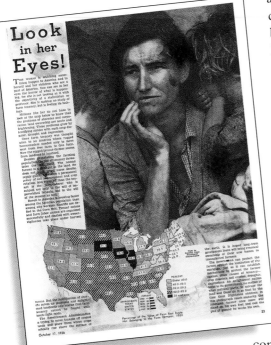

Dorothea Lange's famous photograph Migrant Mother *conveys powerfully the misery of a 32-year-old mother of seven children struggling to make ends meet in California.*

represent a challenge to the system. Okie housing was just one of the areas where the state's liberal and conservative forces clashed over the treatment of the migrants. The Okies were increasingly subject to resentment from other Californians.

ANTI-OKIE RESENTMENT

The thirties brought just over one million migrants to California, fewer than either the preceding or following decades. Yet the Okies, particularly those in agricultural areas, aroused more resentment than the migrants of the twenties and forties, who were absorbed into the state with little difficulty. A strident campaign began to get rid of the Okies. As increasing numbers of these poorer migrants

arrived, the state actively dissuaded them with billboard warnings. At the height of anti-Okie hysteria a billboard on Highway 66 outside Tulsa, Oklahoma, read:

"NO JOBS in California
If YOU are looking for
work—KEEP OUT
6 men for Every Job
No State Relief
Available for
Non-Residents."

The very name "Okie" and its variant, "Arkie," were derogatory and condescending, meaning little more than white trash. The growers stereotyped the migrants as shiftless, lazy, and promiscuous, adjectives they had previously reserved for their nonwhite, non-American workforce. For their own part the migrants resented the label. Texans and Missourians were quick to point out that they did not come from Oklahoma, and Oklahomans defined an Okie as a Dust Bowl migrant. One of the earliest migrants, a foreman of a lemon orchard, described himself thus: "I'm from Oklahoma, but I got here a little ahead of the

rest of them, so now I'm a Californian." The label Okie only stopped being an embarrassment in the late 1960s.

As the decade drew to a close, anti-Okie fever increased, orchestrated by the conservative Associated Farmers' Association. When Roosevelt's administration ignored their demands to send the Okies home, the Associated Farmers started a campaign to undermine the Okies in the eyes of the rest of the state. They claimed the migrants had only moved to California for relief benefits, that they were work shy, uneducated, and therefore easy prey for the Communist Party.

In reality all Okies had to wait a year before they could claim relief, and they were eager to work. In 1938 the farm wage in Oklahoma was $1.35 and did not include housing, while in California the wage of $2.95 also included a housing allowance. Relief payments, on the other hand, were traditionally low: Until 1938 the state was staunchly Republican, and the growers had been able to keep relief payments low, with the follow-on effect that workers would accept lower wages.

The growers might have succeeded in persuading the rest of the state that the Okies were lazy

Bum Blockade

On February 4, 1936, the Los Angeles police chief positioned 150 of his police officers at the state's entry points in a "bum blockade." The police searched and evicted any nonresident trying to enter the state for several weeks until they were stopped because California's attorney general declared the blockade to be unconstitutional. It infringed the basic civil right of freedom of movement. For all its illegality, however, the bum blockade was important in raising the whole issue of what to do with the transients and migrants who were flocking to California.

A demonstration in front of San Francisco's city hall by members of the Worker's Alliance protesting cuts in the relief appropriation by the United States Congress, 1939.

good-for-nothings had it not been for events in 1938 and 1939 that turned public opinion against them in favor of the Okies. In January 1938 the blue skies of San Joaquin Valley turned dark. Severe floods hit the region, washing away the ditch banks and, with them, the camps. The Okies were left homeless, hungry, cold, and sick. Newspapers flocked to the region to capture images of the homeless migrants huddled under trees. As photographs appeared across the state, the Okies caught the public imagination. The realization that the Okies had been living in miserable conditions for years

shocked the American public, who were now eager to help. An Emergency Flood Relief Committee was formed to provide blankets, clothing, cash, tobacco, and candy for the migrants. Pressed by public opinion the federal government was also moved to act: Between February and October 1938 it supported 50,000 migrants with its grant-in-aid program.

DWINDLING WORK AND WAGES
At the same time, the second Agricultural Adjustment Act reduced California's cotton acreage from 618,000 to under 400,000 acres. Fewer pickers were needed and, since the floods had destroyed many other crops, there was less work available. By 1940 farm wages were lower than they had been in 1933 thanks to the oversupply of labor.

DEMOCRAT VICTORY
The gubernatorial election of 1938 altered the political landscape of California. Throughout the decade the state had been dominated by a coalition of the wealthiest farmers and local businessmen, who had controlled relief, labor, and welfare policy.

Many Okies had registered to vote when they arrived in California because registration was the proof of residency needed to qualify for relief. Increases in voter registration were an indicator of migrant settlement across the state. In San Francisco voter registration increased by barely 1 percent between 1936 and 1938. In comparison, it jumped 35 percent in Madera County and 22 percent in Kern County.

The federal aid that followed the floods of 1938 increased the loyalty of the Okies—traditional Democrats—to Roosevelt and the New Deal administration. In 1938 they helped vote in Democrat candidate Culbert Olson, swinging the balance away from the Republicans for the first time. Olson received his highest percentage of votes in Kern, Madera, and Fresno counties and was more successful in the upper San Joaquin Valley than in his home county of Los Angeles. However, the Okies had not won the victory alone; there were not enough of them to account for Olson's 200,000-vote margin over the Republican governor Merriam. The valley counties, previously supporters of the large growers, had also turned liberal Democrat. The growers blamed the Okies for the swing and focused their anger on them.

Tackling Interstate Migration
The new governor recognized three key issues raised by Okie migration. Olson wanted to

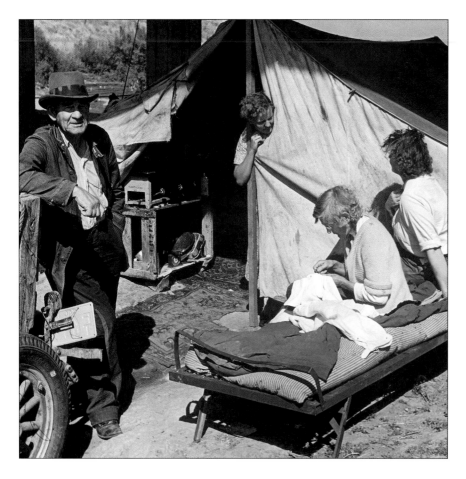

This Okie family was one of many interviewed by author John Steinbeck as research for his novel The Grapes of Wrath.

address the problem of interstate migration, plan how to deal with the problem of relief, and investigate the state of California's agribusiness as revealed by the Okies' arrival. His administration's solutions widened the gap between it and the conservative elements that still controlled the legislature. Olson proposed reforms such as public ownership of private utilities, reorganization of the tax structure, repeal of infringements of civil liberties, production-for-use, and increased social welfare activities.

Within two weeks of Olson taking office in January 1939 it was clear that he stood little success of getting any legislation passed. The

conservative-minded legislature blocked every proposal. Indeed, in spring 1940 the state passed the Relief Appropriation Act, raising the period of eligibility for relief from one to three years. Anyone who entered the state after June 1, 1940, would have to be resident for five years before they could apply for state aid.

STEINBECK'S WRATHFUL GRAPES

In 1939 John Steinbeck published *The Grapes of Wrath*, his story of the fictional Joad family's migration from Oklahoma to California (see Volume 5, Chapter 6, "Chroniclers of the Great Depression"). The novel was the result of extensive fieldwork between 1936 and 1938 into the treatment of the Okies in California. Steinbeck was impressed by their physical and emotional stamina, and his novel

was a powerful plea for a fairer future for the migrants. His portrayal of the greedy, unscrupulous ranch owners infuriated the real growers, particularly when the federal government announced that it would look into the California labor situation. The Oklahomans were also displeased at the depiction of the Joads as a typical family; Steinbeck's portrait of them as dirty and uneducated was not a flattering one.

The book became a national sensation, and the subsequent film version added to the nationwide attention now focused on the Okies. The nation could not believe that its fellow white citizens, who had moved from one state to another to start a new life, had been denied the opportunity by a feudal agricultural business and greedy ranch owners.

News reporters flocked to California to prove that the novel was telling the truth. Prior to the publication of *The Grapes of Wrath* few articles had been written about the migrants in nonacademic national magazines. Suddenly they were all over the nation's media. Roosevelt took note of the public's outrage and, in one of his fireside chats, suggested relocating the migrants to land in the Columbia River basin. The president failed to explain what would then happen to the unpicked crops in California.

With the president eager to see some action, the administration sent a procession of people, including Eleanor Roosevelt, to verify Steinbeck's book. The California legislature itself still could not agree on how to solve the Okie problem. The only solution it proposed was a report on the situation. The Tolan Committee Report comprised the largest collection of facts on

Sinclair's Gaffe

During the 1934 gubernatorial campaign the Democrat candidate Upton Sinclair (1878–1968)—famous as the author of *The Jungle*—wanting to help the less fortunate, committed political suicide when he joked: "If I am elected, about half the unemployed in the whole country will climb aboard freight trains and head for California." The anti-Sinclair opposition maximized the capital to be gained from such a gaffe. Hollywood's anti-Sinclair forces made "newsreels" of tramps marching to California, and the press printed photographs of west-bound jalopies with "Sinclair for Governor" stickers. Sinclair was not elected.

migrant problems in the United States. Congressman Tolan and four colleagues traveled thousands of miles and collected 500 testimonies in California and elsewhere. By the time the report was published, however, events had made it virtually irrelevant.

NEW WAVE OF MIGRATION

By the time the Tolan Committee arrived in California itself in 1940, it found only a reduced number of Okies picking the crops. Once they had saved enough money for the trip to the cities, most Okies were now leaving the fields for the newly constructed factories of the defense industries. The outbreak of World War II in Europe in 1939 created thousands of new jobs and began a wave of migration to California that would bring two and a half million new arrivals. Their arrival prompted no cries of complaint, and they were absorbed into Californian life without question or protest.

A movie still from the film version of Steinbeck's The Grapes of Wrath, *showing members of the Joad family. The migrants became collectively known as Joads.*

Back in the valleys the Okies' misery finally came to an end as money washed into the state to feed the huge war industries. For every Okie who arrived between 1935 and 1940 two migrants came during the war. For every migrant—Okies and others—who arrived between 1930 and 1940 three came in the 1940s. Many were as poor as the Okies had been, but no one minded: There was plenty of work to go around.

5

CRIME IN THE DEPRESSION

During the Depression crime ranged from petty stealing committed by desperate people struggling through times of poverty to hoodlums and gangs capable of serious crimes such as murder and kidnapping.

ELIMINATE CRIME IN THE SLUMS THROUGH HOUSING

NEW YORK CITY HOUSING AUTHORITY

FIORELLO H. LaGUARDIA MAYOR   LANGDON W. POST COMMISS

The Great Depression changed the nature of crime: Some crimes related to the nation's economic straits; others were linked to Prohibition and the market for illegal alcohol. Still others sprang from some people's inherently criminal nature. As the Great Depression wore on, progressive thinkers emphasized social control as the key to fighting the crime that emerged from America's industrialized cities; lawlessness seemed to threaten capitalist society itself. Old laws were revoked and new laws created. The nature of policing changed, too, most notably with the rise of the Federal Bureau of Investigation (FBI). Some observers detect another change in the thirties in the attitude of Americans to criminals. In parts of society that had lost all faith in authority, some people saw the criminals who defied the system, stole from

A poster campaigning for better housing to end crime in the city slums. During the Great Depression people without welfare relief were sometimes driven to commit crimes through sheer desperation.

African American convicts sing as they work in a woodyard in Reed Camp, South Carolina, 1934.

banks and businesses, and fought against the authorities as representatives of the little people struggling through hard times. Many others saw them as nothing more than greedy, vicious thugs.

1. CRIMES OF POVERTY

Some crime, particularly in the early years of the Depression, merely sprang from poverty. Many of the starving committed what might be called acts of desperation rather than crimes as they tried to survive at a time when the government provided no welfare relief. When the funds donated to charitable agencies dried up in the second and third years of the Depression, petty crime increased.

An illegal squatter makes coffee in the makeshift kitchen of his home in an abandoned warehouse in Caruthersville, Missouri.

Often such thievery might be limited to an individual woman stealing fruit off a stand while the clerk's back was turned. At other times groups of women and men—all desperate to feed themselves and their families—attacked grocery stores en masse. In Okla-

Illegal Cooperatives

The vast majority of impoverished Americans never stole. Some of the destitute, however, sought creative solutions to their poverty that skirted the legal formalities of establishing and running a real business. In Seattle the Unemployed Citizens League created a cooperative of shoemakers, carpenters, tailors, and laborers who traded their skills with those who fished, grew fruit, harvested vegetables, and could swap goods. It is estimated that over 40,000 Seattlers, or 13,000 families, cooperated in this paralegal economy. By the end of 1932, 30 states housed more than 100 such cooperatives.

homa City, for example, 500 men and women raided a downtown grocery store in January 1931. Not only did they commit the crime in daylight; the store was located practically next to City Hall. Police arrested 26 of the thieves. In another incident 500 Michigan men, having been denied shelter at the lodge for the unemployed because they had insufficient funds, raided grocery stores in the summer of 1931. That same year the hungry of the Twin Cities attacked groceries in both Minneapolis and Saint Paul, stealing meat, groceries, and canned goods. Miners in the Blue Ridge Mountains smashed store-front windows, climbed in, and stole food for their empty bellies. It was common in small towns and big cities alike to see normally law-abiding citizens stealing food.

VAGRANCY

As well as food the destitute required shelter. If they had been evicted from their homes, they often had nowhere to go. When the homeless built their Hooverville shantytowns in

cities across the nation, they were forced to break laws governing building homes on public property. There were too many to be arrested. Sleeping on a park bench or in a bus stop or subway tunnel, however, did lead to incarceration. Newspapers across the nation reported that police often arrested vagrants with reluctance and would delay presenting them to the judge so as to ensure that the vagrant received a good night's sleep in

A worker cleans up after a raid on the offices of a Long Island City lumber company in 1933. After trussing the watchman the robbers broke open this large safe and got away with cash, weapons, and coin collections worth a total of around $10,000.

Hobos riding an empty freight car to southern California in 1934. Millions of hobos stole rides on the railroads in the Depression.

the jail and some food. However, a few homeless people in Chicago sought shelter in a way that the police treated far less kindly. Fifty-five men were arrested for stealing a four-story building that they had dismantled brick by brick.

In mining communities in Pennsylvania and Wyoming police arrested unemployed miners who worked without pay but took the coal home with them. Sympathetic juries acquitted the accused.

HOBOS ON FREIGHT TRAINS

Police tried to round up the men, women, and children who illegally rode train cars. Because millions of hobos rode the rails in this way, many cities tried to deal with them leniently. First-time offenders might be let off if they were very young and showed no signs of having been incarcerated

Three men help Harry Bennett, head of Ford Motor Company's secret service staff, into the back of an automobile after he was injured in the 1932 riot at the River Rouge Plant in Dearborn, Michigan.

before. Jail sentences for first-time offenders were only 30 days, but repeat offenders in some states worked on a chain gang. The shackles used to chain prisoners together rubbed the lower legs and ankles raw: When hobos were arrested, police checked their legs to determine whether they were repeat offenders. In Florida, whose warm climate attracted many hobos, repeat offenders could expect to serve for three months if caught and convicted of stealing a ride on the railroad.

JOBLESS DEMONSTRATORS

Business owners grew increasingly alarmed as they watched unemployed, homeless, and destitute Americans take matters into their own hands. They feared that the

United States would be plunged into class warfare as capitalism failed. Such business leaders looked to FDR to stave off a potential communist revolution and save American capitalism.

Unemployed protesters were often treated as criminal revolutionaries. In March 1930, 35,000 jobless demonstrators in New York City's Union Square were set upon by police using clubs. Reporters at the scene noted the amount of blood splattered on buildings from

the bludgeoning of men and women of all ages. A similar mêlée occurred in Cleveland the same month. In March 1932, 3,000 former auto workers in Dearborn, Michigan, were hosed down with ice-cold water and fired on with machine guns when they marched peacefully to present their former employers with a petition for new jobs. Police protecting the plant killed four of the crowd. Riots sprang up in Philadelphia, Los Angeles, Chicago, and Seattle as the jobless gathered to try and figure out how to deal with the hard times and petitioned local governments for help.

2. POLITICAL CRIMES

The strain the Great Depression put on society made many people fearful of the breakdown of democratic politics. The largest specter was communism, but in the 1930s right-wing extremism was also seen as a threat (see Volume 4, Chapter 1, "Left vs. Right"). People perceived threats everywhere. Former president Herbert Hoover, for example, worried that government regulation of welfare and other policies were close to communism and accused Roosevelt of introducing a form of communism to the United States.

Intellectual Criminals?

In the August 1932 issue of *Harper's* a distinguished economic historian, George Soule, tried to allay the fears of many Americans concerning the rise in crimes committed by the unemployed. In "Are We Going to Have a Revolution?" he argued that while the actions of the starving might appear to be revolutionary, it was intellectuals who should be feared, not the workers. The workers, he argued, were smashing windows because they were hungry, not because they wanted a new form of government. Nevertheless, America's elite looked at starving mobs and saw criminals.

Mounted police officers charge communists and unemployed demonstrators on a hunger march at City Hall Plaza, Washington, D.C., in January 1931.

HOOVER AND COMMUNISM

In 1931, as crowds broke into stores and stormed government offices around the country, Hoover opposed a reduction in the armed forces. They had to be available in case of revolution, he insisted. In 1932, when federal employees took a 10 percent pay cut, Hoover excused the armed forces to maintain morale. Just weeks before he lost the 1932 election, he called in the Army to move a Hooverville in Anacostia, Washington, D.C. It was filled with veterans of World War I requesting their bonus pay (see Volume 3, Chapter 1, "Tough in the City"). Hoover justified the violent eviction by agreeing with his military leaders' claims that the veterans were led by communists.

ROOSEVELT AND EXTREMISM

Roosevelt's administration also pursued communists as criminals, lumping pro-German Nazis and pro-Italian fascists into the same category of threat. These three types of "criminals" were pursued as "un-American," and the United State Congress formed a special committee to investigate their activities, beginning in 1934.

Communist cells undoubtedly did exist in the United States; but as extremism grew in Europe (see Volume 6, Chapter 2, "The Victory of Authoritarianism"), the House Un-American Activities Committee paid more attention to right-wing extremism. Americans across the nation were practicing goose-step marches and straight-armed salutes as they admired their counterparts in Italy and Germany. Wearing brown shirts as uniforms, the German-American Bund hoped to bring the "fatherland's" Nazism to America. Black-shirted Italian-American fascists referred to their ghetto communities as "colonies" of mother Italy and spoke of uniting with Mussolini's forces in a new Roman Empire. The American Silver Shirt Legion appealed to citizens who believed that the principles of racial supremacy and global-military authority expressed by European fascists could be tailored to American interests. The minority of Americans who joined such organizations were branded as criminals under the Espionage and Sedition Acts left over from World War I and prosecuted when the nation went to war in the 1940s.

RACE CRIMES

Extremist politics were also advocated by the Ku Klux Klan. Although the Klan theoretically opposed Nazis and fascists, they

Redefining Crime

Just as America's race crimes diminished after the Roosevelts entered the White House in 1933, petty crimes such as stealing food diminished, too. Franklin Roosevelt's New Deal policies of direct aid and work relief and his attempts to build a planned economy for a diverse nation helped reduce the occurrence of crimes born out of destitution because people's lives improved. The New Deal also passed new laws and set up new agencies that changed the very definition of certain crimes: The formation of the Securities and Exchange Commission regulated the stock market for the first time, the repeal of Prohibition ended the violent gangsterism associated with bootlegged alcohol, and the creation of the Federal Bureau of Investigation ushered in a new era of crime prevention.

Members of the white supremacist organization, the Ku Klux Klan, parade in ceremonial robes and hoods. Racial hatred—not only toward African Americans, but also toward Catholics, Jews, and all immigrants—branded the Ku Klux Klan as criminals.

preached similar militancy and racial hatred toward African Americans. Although the Klan had diminished since its peak membership of five million in the mid-1920s, it remained active in both the rural South and the urban North. The 1930s saw African American schools burned and successful southern blacks forced to move to northern cities. In the cities, however, the Klan argued vigorously that the few jobs available should go to "native" American Christian whites. When African Americans working on the Illinois Central Railroad were methodically murdered, the press believed that the criminals had been motivated by the Klan's racist ideology.

FDR and Race

Roosevelt's ability to help minorities was limited by his reliance on the support of Southern Democrats who opposed antiracist legislation (see Volume 5, Chapter 2, "Equality for Some"). FDR, however, still appointed African Americans, both men and women, to positions of power and included all races and ethnicities in his New Deal policies. Eleanor Roosevelt celebrated diversity more visibly, publicly rejecting her membership in the Daughters of the American Revolution when they refused their performance hall to the world-renowned opera singer Marian Anderson because she was an African American (see Volume 2, Chapter 3, "The Roosevelts: A New Style"). When Roosevelt discovered his nominee as a Supreme Court justice had once been a member of the Klan, the judge renounced his membership and apologized to the nation. Thus, together, the Roosevelts helped set a new stage that discouraged racial crimes.

3. BUSINESS CRIME

The Securities and Exchange Commission was created in 1934 in response to the "white-collar" activities used to propel the stock market to new heights in the 1920s, many of which had been dishonest. The false claims routinely made by some businessmen or brokers to encourage investors to part with their money were now made criminal offenses.

The dramatic rise in stock prices in the 1920s reflected other dishonest practices that were outlawed in the New Deal. Inves-

A group of criminals guard their private beer-brewing hide-out in 1932. During the Prohibition era it was illegal to make liquor to sell. Since millions of people still wanted to drink alcohol, however, a huge criminal trade came into existence to supply it to them.

tors used ploys that artificially elevated stock prices. Several individuals might form a group and continually outbid each other, day after day, paying more and more for stock in a company that perhaps was not worth a high stock price. As other investors watched the price go up, they became encouraged to buy the stock and so reap the profits. In this way the price would climb to dizzy heights unrelated to the real value of the stock, until the group of insiders all sold together at the same time. Then the stock would rapidly fall

The St. Valentine's Day massacre, in which Capone's gang killed seven members of a rival gang, won him control of Chicago's underworld.

to its original price, or lower, leaving the newer investors out of pocket. Many dishonest brokers and investors fled to Europe after the market crashed, outside of United States jurisdiction. The Securities Exchange Act (SEA) made such practices illegal, and "white-collar" criminals were prosecuted by the Roosevelt administration.

4. GANGSTERS AND PROFESSIONAL CRIME

The Great Depression was a heyday for gangsters in the United States. While the ending of Prohibition in 1933 undermined the trade in illegal liquor, a whole rogues gallery of criminals came to the forefront of the popular imagination, including Bonnie and Clyde, John Dillinger, and Machine Gun Kelly. Phrases such as "Public Enemy Number One" reflected an almost admiring attitude toward such outlaws. As FBI boss J. Edgar Hoover and others were quick to point out, there was nothing to admire about these brutal, selfish criminals. Roosevelt suggested they be called "public rats."

In 1933 Roosevelt and Congress ended the prohibition on alcoholic beverages that had been in place since the Eighteenth Amendment of 1920. In doing so, he also undermined the illegal trade in liquor. For more than a decade that business had been in the hands of organized crime. Among the most notorious Prohibition criminals was Al Capone (1899–1947), known as Scarface .

Italian-American gangster Al Capone was born in Naples, Italy, in 1899 and raised in Brooklyn, New York. He left school early and, by 1927, was turning over an income of more than $100 million from his dealings in illegal liquor, gambling, and prostitution in Chicago. During the following years, in a series of gang wars, he eliminated his rivals. His criminal activities caught up with him eventually, and in 1931 he was sentenced to 11 years in prison for income-tax evasion. He was released on parole after eight years, suffering from brain disease brought on by untreated syphilis, and died in 1947 at the age of 48.

AL CAPONE

Born in 1899, Al Capone became a teenage gang member in New York. When Prohibition came into force in the early 1920s, he was a lieutenant in the Colosimo mob, providing the beer and liquor Americans wanted. He once told his critics: "I give the people what they want." Capone rough-handed anyone who got in his way. In 1925 he became the boss of the Colosimo/Torrio gang and stayed in power by methodically eliminating the competition.

St. Valentine's Day Massacre

On February 14, 1929, Capone's gang dressed as police officers and pretended to roust members of the Bugs Moran gang, a rival mob in Chicago. The "police" lined the hoodlums against a garage wall and opened fire, killing seven men in what the papers dubbed the "St. Valentine's Day Massacre." Capone, in Florida at the time, was deeply implicated. He was called to Chicago to testify in the court case but refused.

Capone submitted a doctor's note affirming that he suffered from poor health and could not travel from Miami to the Chicago court. Agents of the BOI (see box, page 90), however, showed that Capone had traveled to vacation destinations throughout his allegedly debilitating sickness. They arrested the mobster, who quickly posted bail and was released from custody. Within a few weeks Capone found himself behind bars again, this time for carrying concealed weapons. He served nine months in jail.

Guilty of Tax Evasion

With Capone behind bars, the U.S. Treasury Department collected evidence that he had avoided paying almost a quarter of a million dollars in taxes. Capone, his brother "Bottles," and "Greasy Thumb" Guzik were found guilty of tax evasion in 1931. Al Capone, already notorious in American popular culture, first served his time in the federal prison in Atlanta and in 1934 was transferred to the ultimate penitentiary for criminals of the Great Depression: Alcatraz (see box, page 92).

LINDBERGH BABY KIDNAPPING

One of the most infamous crimes of the Depression was the kidnapping of the baby son of the aviator Charles Lindbergh (1902–1974). Lindbergh had become a national hero when he made the first solo flight across the Atlantic in 1927 (see Volume 1, Chapter 4, "The Roaring Twenties"). Lindbergh's baby was taken from his Hopewell, N.J., home on the evening of March 1, 1932. The response reflected Lindbergh's status. Next day the U.S. Attorney General, the director of the Bureau of Investigation, the New Jersey State Police, and the New York City Police met to pool efforts.

Ransom Notes

The Lindbergh family received ransom notes for six weeks after the kidnapping. The kidnapper corresponded in notes sent via cab drivers to third-party members of the investigation. In turn, the family responded in messages published in the local newspaper and through an intermediary, Dr. Condon. Condon, a retired school principal, volunteered to help the national hero recover his baby and met with the kidnapper to pay the ransom. Condon's close observation of the kidnapper played an important part in the eventual prosecution of the man accused of stealing the baby. The infant was found dead after the ransom had been paid. Shocked by the crime, however, the United States Congress made kidnapping a federal offense, allowing it to be enforced by the BOI.

Gathering Evidence

The BOI spent the rest of 1932 through 1934 piecing together clues to the crime in an early example of criminal profiling. They studied the handwriting of the ransom notes. They took apart the ladder used to steal the baby through an upstairs window and noted the techniques of construction that might identify the person who built it. They compiled a composite of the probable kidnapper based on extensive interviews with Dr. Condon. When they put all the evidence together, they believed they were looking for a German-born immigrant carpenter.

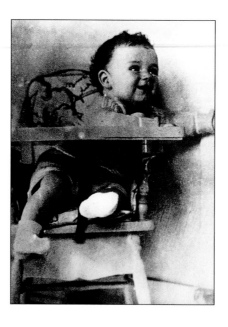

The 20-month-old son of Charles Lindbergh smiles from his highchair in 1932, shortly before he was kidnapped.

The Search Narrows

Meanwhile, banks in the New York City and northern New Jersey areas looked out for the marked bills used in the ransom payoff. On May 2, 1933, nearly $3,000 in $10 bills surfaced at the Federal Reserve Bank of New York. The BOI began noting the banks where ransom notes were discovered and focused their search on New York City. As they interviewed bank tellers and store clerks who received the bills, they sharpened their picture of the man to whom Dr. Condon had handed the ransom. The publicity given to the case, the circulation of the artist's impression, and the fact that much of the ransom had been paid with "gold certificate" bills that were no longer in circulation put citizens on the alert. On September 15, 1934, a man fitting the picture handed a gas-station attendant a gold certificate $10 bill. The attendant jotted the man's license plate number on the bill. When the authorities tracked

down the car, they arrived at a home in the Bronx. The German-American who lived there had just taken an early retirement from his career as a carpenter; the remaining ransom money was hidden in his garage. Bruno Richard Hauptmann was electrocuted for the crime nearly two years later.

MACHINE GUN KELLY

George Kelly Barnes (1895–1954), better known as "Machine Gun" Kelly for his favorite weapon, became a household name in 1933, but his life of crime started with bootlegging during Prohibition. By 1929 he had been jailed twice for smuggling liquor. His crimes were local and not associated with the big-time crime of gangsters such as Capone, but his second arrest put

The Bureau of Investigation

The Federal Bureau of Investigation (FBI) did not exist yet and would not until 1935. Its predecessor, the Bureau of Investigation (BOI), contained a small force of agents who were not even authorized to carry guns and fought only a few federal crimes—and these it fought in competition with other federal bureaus. The Department of the Treasury, for example, held jurisdiction over violations of Prohibition. The BOI focused on helping to bring Al Capone to justice in 1929 by gathering the evidence needed to prove the gangster had treated the justice system with contempt.

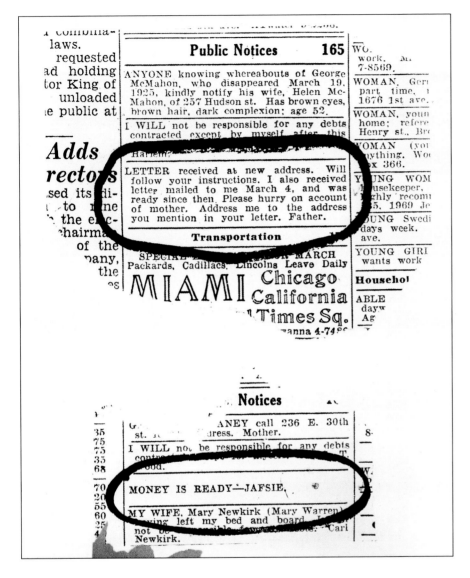

Two announcements that appeared in New York City newspapers during the attempt to pay the Lindbergh baby's kidnapper the ransom money.

him in federal prison at Leavenworth, where he came into contact with more notorious gangsters, from whom he was eager to learn. After serving two years, Kelly left Leavenworth and quickly became much more than just a bootlegger. He formed partnerships with murderers and bank robbers throughout the early 1930s and associated particularly with gangsters in the Twin Cities, Chicago, and Texas.

Botched Kidnapping

Kelly first ventured into kidnapping in Indiana in 1932. His victim, a banker's son, convinced Kelly that his family could not raise the ransom, but that he would pay it himself, if set free. Kelly released him, but never received any money.

Later that year Kelly tried his hand at bank robbery, which proved more successful. He robbed banks in Washington, Mississippi, and Texas.

Urschel Kidnapping

In early 1933 Kelly decided to try kidnapping again in partnership with his wife, Kathryn, whose support of her husband extended even to buying the machine gun for which he became famous. The Kellys invited a criminal associate, Albert Bates, to join them, and on July 22, 1933, they invaded the Oklahoma City home of Charles Urschel, a wealthy oil magnate. Things went poorly from the start. When Kelly broke in, he found two men playing cards. He kidnapped both because he did not know which was the intended victim. He later released Urschel's friend, after searching their wallets for identification. He confidently took the right man to a hide-out on a Texas ranch.

Things seemed to be going well. Urschel was a perfect victim. He cooperated with the criminals as they decided on a ransom amount and delivery method. During the entire time he was a captive Urschel chatted with his captors. On July 30, with $200,000 ransom in his hands, Kelly took Urschel back to Oklahoma and released him.

Police Raid

As soon as he got home, Urschel was ready to work with federal agents hunting for Kelly. Urschel had cleverly directed his friendly conversations with his captors to issues that would help locate their hide-out. His kidnappers told him the time of day when Urschel noted airplanes overhead, for example. He had also memorized pieces of their conversations that discussed soil conditions and the history of agriculture in the region. The information Urschel provided allowed the Bureau to consult airplane schedules and crop reports that led them to the Shannon ranch in Texas. By the time agents raided the ranch, Kelly had already fled. The agents arrested the Shannons and

Alcatraz

The U.S. Justice Department designed Alcatraz to be the prison of prisons for the worst criminals of the Great Depression. The island had served as a jail for years, the U.S. Army using it as a military prison for its worst offenders from 1868 to 1933, when it became a federal prison. Called "the Rock" because it contains almost no soil to allow vegetation to grow, the island's climate seemed to deter human life too: It has no freshwater and, located in the middle of San Francisco Bay, often sits in fog surrounded by torrent currents of ice-cold water. It would be difficult for anyone to get off the island, which made it an appropriate site when the Bureau wanted to build an escape-proof prison. When the U.S.

An aerial view of Alcatraz prison in San Francisco Bay, California, in the midthirties. It rises 130ft (40m) above the water and measures 1,755ft (535m) in length.

Army transferred Alcatraz to the Justice Department in late 1933, the prison was renovated with new locking devices, stronger cell-door bars, and new guard towers. It opened for business in July 1934, and Al Capone entered it the following month.

initiated the first trial under the new Lindbergh kidnapping law. It would not be long before they captured Kelly, too.

Kelly Arrest

As Kelly and his wife crisscrossed the nation, robbing and killing, they began spending the ransom money they had exchanged for Urschel. Just as in the Lindbergh case, the bills had been marked. By September the Bureau had tracked Kelly to Memphis, where they easily captured the pair. In an uneventful arrest by Depression-era standards agents broke into the Kellys' room, found them hungover, and arrested them. Kelly apparently exclaimed, "Don't shoot, G-men!" The phrase, which he explained as

being short for "government men," became a popular name for federal agents. Kathryn went to prison until 1958. Kelly spent time in Alcatraz and died in prison in 1954. Their accomplice Bates was captured soon after the Kellys and sent to Alcatraz.

GILLIS AND CHASE

Joining Bates and Kelly on "the Rock" in 1934 was John Paul Chase. Chase had shared his criminal career with Lester Gillis, better known to the public as "Baby Face" Nelson. The pair had robbed and killed together; but when the law caught up with them, only Chase survived.

The ill-fated Gillis had lived a stereotypical life of crime for which gangsters were infamous. Before

he even celebrated his 15th birthday, an Illinois court convicted him of auto theft. He spent two years in a boys' home and, after a short time on parole, landed back in confinement for another auto theft. Upon release he married Helen Wawzynak and graduated to bank robberies.

On February 17, 1932, "Baby Face" Nelson escaped from the Illinois prison system while in transfer to stand trial in a second bank robbery case. On the run westward he teamed up with bootlegger John Chase, and the two soon built a racket supplying liquor to thirsty Californians. Nelson's wife joined him as he and Chase roamed the West, allegedly killing several people who got in their way.

Gillis, Chase, and the Dillinger Gang

By early 1934 "Baby Face," his wife, and Chase had joined the infamous John Dillinger (1903–1934) and his gang in Illinois. When the BOI raided the gang, "Baby Face" escaped, but police captured his wife. As Helen Gillis awaited her release on parole, her husband added the murder of police agents to his list of crimes. Within six months he had killed five police officers and

Bruno Hauptmann's garage, where the ransom was hidden. The insert shows the piece of timber in which some of the money was hidden.

three federal agents. He and Chase joined Dillinger in a bank robbery in June; but when agents shot Dillinger dead the following month, they laid low. By November, however, the Bureau had picked up their trail and found them in a stolen car. Nelson and Chase fired on the agents from their car while Helen Gillis ambushed the agents from the side of the road. "Baby Face" died in the shootout, and agents captured his widow; Chase fled to California, but the next month he was recognized by former acquaintances who turned him in to the authorities. In March 1935 an Illinois court tried a

Hoover and the FBI

The BOI became the Federal Bureau of Investigation (FBI) in 1935. The director of both, J. Edgar Hoover (1895–1972), was a national hero. The New York *World-Telegram* wrote in 1936, "Pick a small boy these days and ask him who…in the world he wants to be and ten to one he will reply—J. Edgar Hoover." "The Director" got the job in 1924, and one of his first acts was to fire about a third of the agents and institute tough new recruiting policies to make sure that his 600 G-men were as incorruptible as himself. In the early 1930s the BOI remained a little-known federal department. In 1932 Congress, at Hoover's urging, increased the number of crimes classed as federal, leaving them open to BOI investigation.

As his agents achieved some spectacular successes, the nondrinking, non-smoking Hoover himself proved a skilled self-publicist. He crusaded against criminals, whose numbers he put at anything between 500,000 and 3.5 million. By 1936 some people were concerned that Hoover's arrogance and unaccountability had turned the FBI into a secret police force. One Senator told him, "It seems to me your department is just running wild." Despite widespread criticism, Hoover kept the job until his death in 1972.

"Machine Gun" Kelly being escorted from Memphis jail in 1933 by police officers wearing fedoras and carrying machine guns.

citizen for the murder of a federal agent for the first time in history. Chase was found guilty and sent to Alcatraz.

JOHN DILLINGER

John Dillinger shared with the other gangsters of his era the reputation for seeing what he wanted and taking it. His particularly brazen crimes earned him a reputation as one of the most infamous criminals of the Depression. He and his gang murdered 10 men, robbed banks, broke jails, and wounded anyone who got in their way.

Escape from Jail

Dillinger captured the public imagination in particular because it seemed impossible to contain him. Shortly after his May 1933 robbery of a bank in Ohio, Dayton police arrested Dillinger and placed him in jail. He planned the escape of several of his colleagues, who returned to the prison and freed him. The number of victims killed by Dillinger's gang rose over the next year as they committed

Dewey and the Mobsters

Thomas Dewey (1902–1971), New York special prosecutor, led the city's fight against organized crime. Mobster Dutch Schultz, shown here, planned to have Dewey assassinated in October 1935. Instead, Schultz was himself gunned down in a restaurant by two hitmen working for the top Mafia leader, Charles "Lucky" Luciano. Luciano figured that Dewey's death would intensify the war on the gangs.

Dewey caught up with Luciano in 1936, and he was given a long jail sentence, along with the rest of his mob, for running a prostitution ring. From 1935 to 1937 Dewey achieved 72 convictions for racketeering. He went on to become governor of New York from 1943 to 1955, twice running unsuccessfully as the Republican presidential candidate.

WANTED

LESTER M. GILLIS,

aliases GEORGE NELSON, "BABY FACE" NELSON, ALEX GILLIS, LESTER GILES,
"BIG GEORGE" NELSON, "JIMMIE", "JIMMY" WILLIAMS .

On June 23, 1934, HOMER S. CUMMINGS, Attorney General of the United States, under the authority vested in him by an Act of Congress approved June 6, 1934, offered a reward of

$5,000.00

for the capture of Lester M. Gillis or a reward of

$2,500.00

for information leading to the arrest of Lester M. Gillis.

DESCRIPTION

Age, 25 years; Height, 5 feet 4-3/4 inches; Weight,
133 pounds; Build, medium; Eyes, yellow and grey
slate; Hair, light chestnut; Complexion, light; Occu-
pation, oiler.

All claims to any of the aforesaid rewards and all questions and disputes that may arise
as among claimants to the foregoing rewards shall be passed upon by the Attorney General and
his decisions shall be final and conclusive. The right is reserved to divide and allocate
portions of any of said rewards as between several claimants. No part of the aforesaid rewards shall be paid to any official or employee of the Department of Justice.

If you are in possession of any information concerning the whereabouts of Lester M. Gillis,
communicate immediately by telephone or telegraph collect to the nearest office of the Division of Investigation, United States Department of Justice, the local offices of which are set
forth on the reverse side of this notice.

The apprehension of Lester M. Gillis is sought in connection with the murder of Special
Agent W. C. Baum of the Division of Investigation near Rhinelander, Wisconsin on April 23,
1934.

JOHN EDGAR HOOVER, DIRECTOR,
DIVISION OF INVESTIGATION,
UNITED STATES DEPARTMENT OF JUSTICE,
WASHINGTON, D. C.

June 25, 1934

A wanted poster for Lester Gillis, also known as "Baby Face" Nelson, and a member of John Dillinger's outlaw gang, June 1934.

carved a fake gun from a block of wood and used it to threaten his way out of jail. He took real guns and fled in the sheriff's car. But when he took the car across state lines, he committed an offense that brought the DOI into the case.

Within six months the Division of Investigation knew Dillinger's whereabouts in Chicago. Befriending one of Dillinger's acquaintances, Ana Cumpanas, also known as Ana Sage, the Bureau promised her reward money and assistance with immigration problems to help them capture the criminal. Cumpanas, who became known as "the Lady in Red," told agents where Dillinger would be on the night of July 22. Agents stationed themselves outside the Biograph Theater in Chicago and waited for Dillinger to enter their trap. At 10:30 P.M., as Dillinger left the theater, he sensed the trap, ran, and drew a gun. Agents fired first, however, and shot him dead.

THE BARKER GANG

The Barker Gang made crime a family business in a career that spanned the twenties and thirties. By the end of the latter decade, however, they were all dead or behind bars.

Herman Barker

Herman Barker had spent the decade of the twenties shooting up saloons in the fashion of his outlaw hero, Jesse James. Arrested for robbery, jailed as a thief, and hunted after breaking out of a Missouri jail, Herman fled to other states. He was arrested for a succession of small crimes: in Montana, Minnesota, Iowa, and

robberies in states all across the nation. Local police could not coordinate a national investigation, so they turned to the Bureau, now the Division of Investigation. Although federal agents could now carry guns, they still had limited jurisdiction, and Dillinger had yet to commit a crime they could prosecute. The federal agents therefore focused

on helping police identify Dillinger and his crowd and make their appearances known to the public.

The federal agents' work paid off when a Tucson, Arizona, firefighter recognized members of Dillinger's gang. In January 1934 Tucson police captured the public enemy and sent him to an "escape proof" jail in Indiana, from which he escaped, nonetheless. Dillinger

Bonnie and Clyde

Clyde Barrow and Bonnie Parker shared a life of crime together from the time they met in 1930 until their deaths in 1934. During that time they committed 13 murders across New Mexico, Texas, Oklahoma, Missouri, and Louisiana, robbing and burglarizing on their way.

In 1930, found guilty of simple burglary, Clyde was sent to a Texas jail. Bonnie smuggled a gun to him, which he used to force his way out. He was recaptured and spent another two years in prison. Upon his release in 1932 he rejoined Bonnie, and they embarked on their murderous spree.

Bonnie and Clyde's criminal inclinations stemmed from a pathological hatred of authority, particularly the system of law and order, which gained them the status of folk heroes among small sections of U.S. society. Most of the people they killed were police officers and prison guards. Newspapers faithfully reported their career of small-time robbery, concentrating on gas stations, restaurants, and small-town banks. Their take was never over $1,500.

The BOI first sought Barrow and Parker for car thefts in 1932. Federal agents still had limited authority, however, so Bonnie and Clyde—the name by which the papers publicized them—were targeted for breaking interstate trafficking laws. As the BOI pursued the pair, however, changes in Washington, D.C., affected how it operated. In 1932 Congress made kidnapping a federal crime, which itself justified the BOI pursuit of the couple, who had kidnapped a woman and man in Louisiana. In June 1933 Roosevelt used the power of Executive Order to consolidate the United States Bureau of Investigation and the Prohibition Bureau into the Division of Investigation (DOI), housed in the Department of Justice. Shortly after the creation of the DOI, Congress authorized its agents to carry sidearms in order to defend themselves.

In April 1934 federal agents narrowed down their search. On the first of the month the duo had killed two highway patrolmen in Texas, and leads suggested that the couple were living nearby in Louisiana. By the end of May agents had narrowed their search to the home of one of the fellow prisoners freed by Clyde during his 1930 Texas jailbreak. Federal agents and police officers staked out an ambush, surrounding a highway they expected Bonnie and Clyde to use. When the couple appeared in their car, officers opened fire in a hail of bullets, killing both occupants. The legend of Bonnie and Clyde was over.

Bonnie Parker playfully points a shotgun at her partner, Clyde Barrow, in 1932. The pair were well-known wanted criminals in a two-year period until their deaths in 1934.

John Dillinger was born in Indianapolis, Indiana, around 1902. He committed his first armed robbery in 1924 and spent nine years in jail. After his release in 1933 his crimes brought him national attention and earned him the title "public enemy number one" from the BOI. Betrayed by an acquaintance, he was shot by federal agents in July 1934.

Tennessee. In 1926 he allegedly robbed a bank in Oklahoma. As authorities looked for Herman, the criminal and his wife cashed checks in Wyoming they had stolen from a Kansas bank. When police stopped Herman's car to inquire about the checks, he killed them and drove off. In doing so, he committed the crime that called in the Bureau—transporting a stolen car across state lines.

With the G-men on his trail Herman's days of crime seemed numbered. Local authorities got to him first. In 1927 he returned to Kansas, where he robbed an icehouse but was surprised by the police. In the shoot-out that ensued, Herman suffered serious

wounds and realized he would be taken into custody. He committed suicide rather than be caught. He did not want to end up like his brother, Lloyd, who was already serving a 25-year sentence at Leavenworth Prison.

Fred Barker

Another Barker brother, Fred, also found himself in Leavenworth. Fred had spent most of the 1920s serving short sentences in local jails around Oklahoma. With each passing year his crimes escalated: First, he was imprisoned for vagrancy, then robbery, then bank robbery. Finally Fred escaped from jail. In 1926 police wounded him in a shootout following an attempted burglary in Kansas City. They captured him and sent him to the Kansas State Prison.

Fred and Alvin Karpis

Serving time with Fred at the prison was Alvin Karpis. Karpis would join Fred and another Barker brother, Albert or "Doc," to create one of the most notorious gangs of Great Depression.

Fred Barker and Alvin Karpis became friends at Leavenworth and, after they were paroled in the spring of 1931, quickly returned to a life of crime. Within a month of Karpis's release the two were arrested in Oklahoma for burgling a jewelry store. The two men did not serve much time: Karpis was quickly paroled, while Barker escaped. They hid out at the Barker homestead in Missouri and spent the next year robbing banks and killing law officers who got in their way.

The Barker-Karpis Gang

As their life of crime escalated, the Barker family had to abandon their homestead. The whole family

was now wanted by local law officials. The Barker gang moved to Minnesota. Committing burglaries, hijacking cars, and holding up citizens, the criminals recruited young gangsters just starting their criminal lives and won the respect of seasoned veterans of crime. Known as "the Barker-Karpis Gang," they crossed state lines and robbed throughout the Mississippi River Valley. Sometimes they netted only a few thousand dollars; other robberies yielded hundreds of thousands of dollars. Killing those who got in their way, sometimes in dramatic shootouts with police in front of the banks, the Barker-Karpis gang dominated the area west of Capone's Chicago.

The gang also turned to kidnapping. In 1934 they extorted a $100,000 ransom for the release of

New Duties for "G-men"

In addition to closing the chapter on another gangster's life, the Division of Investigation's search for John Dillinger opened up a new chapter for federal agents. Congress decided in 1934 that the limited federal authority which agents held should be expanded. They believed that the crimes most associated with Dillinger that were not federal offenses now had to fall under federal jurisdiction. As a result, bank robberies, jailbreaks, and fleeing a state to avoid prosecution became issues that government agents, or "G-men," could handle.

nondescript home in Oklawaha, Florida. G-men tracked them down anyway. Federal agents surrounded the house on January 16, 1935, and demanded the mother and son allow themselves to be arrested peacefully. The answer came in bullets. Ma and Fred had amassed an arsenal, and the ensuing gun battle lasted for hours. Over a thousand bullets flew through the air; and when all went quiet inside the house, federal agents moved in and found the bodies of mother and son. The entire Barker gang was either dead or in federal prison.

THE END OF PROFESSIONAL CRIME

The end of the Barker gang marked the end of the kind of professional crime that had characterized the Great Depression. Professional law enforcement, particularly in the shape of the

Albert Barker, one of the Barker brothers, pictured in jail with chief jailer William Gates of Ramsey County, Minnesota, jail in 1935.

William Hamm, Jr., head of the Hamm's Brewing Company. They laundered the money, frustrating agents' efforts to trace it. But their luck ran out. After kidnapping the president of the Commercial State Bank of St. Paul, the gang's attempts to launder the $200,000 ransom money failed. The Bureau began to close in on the gang, and by 1935 agents began arresting its less prominent members. Although it would take G-men another year to capture Karpis, agents tracing the ransom money found Albert at a Chicago apartment in January 1935 and arrested him. They had just missed his brother, Fred, who had fled to Florida with their mother, Arizona Barker.

Ma Barker

Arizona Barker became known to America as "Ma Barker" or sometimes as "Ma Baker." As the mother of so many criminal sons, she received the blame for raising them poorly. The way she willingly bailed her sons out of jail when they were arrested and moved to new communities when they were paroled suggested that she was deeply involved in their activities. When the Barker-Karpis gang operated out of her home, her name began to appear in arrest warrants and offers of reward money for bringing in the gang.

When federal agents closed in on the gang, Ma Barker and her son Fred settled themselves into a

Ma Barker, 60-year-old mother of the four Barker brothers, pictured with her close friend Arthur Dunlop in 1935.

The bungalow in Oklawaha, Florida, where Fred and Ma Barker were shot after a four-hour gun battle with the FBI.

Bureau of Investigation, later the FBI, had been expanding since 1933. Throughout its many name changes the Bureau had remained true to the principles of its director, J. Edgar Hoover (see box, page 93). The Bureau developed an approach to crimefighting based on diligence and the painstaking collection and analysis of data. Hoover was later criticized for acting without regard to the country's political leaders or the strict letter of the law.

Early in the Depression the government had acknowledged the importance of the federal agents by arming them and in 1934 expanding their jurisdiction. In 1935, the government created the agency that still exists today, the FBI. Although its duties remained similar to those of the BOI and DOI, the name change reflected the agency's tradition of being "the Bureau." With a new name and increased responsibilities came a new level of funding—over $6 million in 1936, more than twice the total when Roosevelt first took office. The Bureau spent the rest of the 1930s fighting some of the most notorious of the era's gangsters. The battle was largely successful. No more names with the infamy of Dillinger or the Barkers emerged after 1935. The tide had turned and news headlines charted the G-men's steady progress in the capture and incarceration of the nation's gangsters.

5. ESPIONAGE

Just as the organized gangster crime of the early and mid-thirties seemed to replace the small-scale crimes of individual desperation of the early years of the Depression, so a new type of crime appeared in the late thirties. In 1936 Roosevelt asked the FBI to obtain information relating to subversive political activities. As political and military tension threatened the balance of power in Europe, the government was more fearful that fifth-column Nazis might cause trouble in the United States. In 1938 federal agents cracked the Rumrich spy case, which had begun in 1935 when U.S. Customs officials had discovered letters and microfilm concealed in a violin case, and indicted 18 individuals for espionage. The FBI went on to take charge of investigating espionage and subversion. J. Edgar Hoover later testified to a congressional committee that the FBI had investigated 19,587 cases of alleged sabotage by German or pro-German agents, of which 2,417 cases proved to be actual sabotage.

6

CONTINUING PLIGHT OF THE FARMER

Early in the Depression government worked to raise agricultural prices; later, new agencies addressed longer-term problems of land conservation and of rural poverty itself. Their planning reflected a traditional idea: that, having provided immediate relief, policies should address recovery and reform.

In the early years of his first term Roosevelt introduced various measures to relieve the problems of farmers (see Chapter 2, "Shadow over the Countryside"). As part of the New Deal farm reforms the Agricultural Adjustment Administration (AAA) of 1933 sought to restore farm prices, which had become seriously depressed due to a critical problem of overproduction and underdistribution. The act restricted the amount of land under cultivation and subsidized farmers to limit their production. Surplus food programs were devised to distribute surplus supplies to those in need.

Roosevelt also tried to address the problem of widespread rural poverty and to ease credit and mortgage problems among debt-ridden farmers. He established various credit and mortgage relief

A Missouri state conservationist advertisement from around 1935. A major part of the government's agricultural program involved soil conservation and general environmental issues.

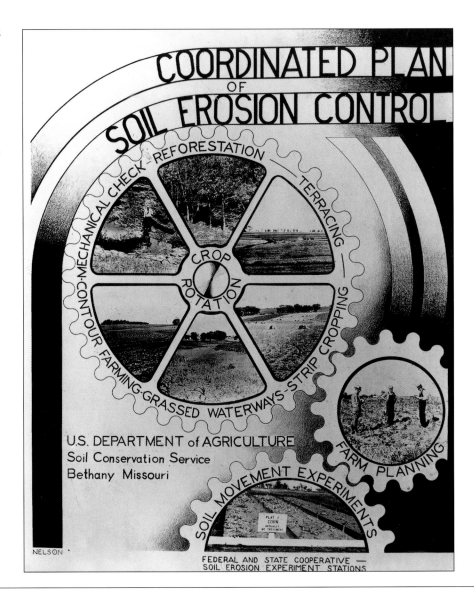

This cartoon shows Chief Justice Charles Evans Hughes kicking over the Agricultural Adjustment Administration. It was ruled unconstitutional in January 1936.

programs to provide loans to farmers in debt. These and other New Deal farm reforms produced encouraging results in Roosevelt's first term, with prices improving and farm income rising by 50 percent. However, the AAA was destined to have a limited life.

1. AAA RULED UNCONSTITUTIONAL

By the time the essential farm relief program of the Roosevelt administration was in place, the Supreme Court had dealt a blow to the New Deal in agriculture (see Volume 4, Chapter 2, "The Supreme Court"). The court had already, in May 1935, ruled the National Industrial Recovery Act illegal. In January 1936 it also ruled that the AAA was unconstitutional. The judgment was handed down by a vote of 6 to 3. What offended the justices in the majority was the levy the AAA

placed on the processors of agricultural goods. Justice Pierce Butler, for the majority, said that to take money from one group for the benefit of another was not a fit use of the federal government's taxing authority.

The majority opinion was also that agricultural policy was a matter for the states, not the federal government. The court ordered the $200 million that had been collected from the agricultural processors to be returned to them. The court, by taking an ax to one of the central legislative achievements of Roosevelt's government and a key weapon in its battle against economic depression, set itself squarely behind right-wing opponents of the New Deal, such as the American Liberty League. That organization had been formed by businessmen in 1934 to oppose government intervention in the free working of the market (see Volume 4, Chapter 4, "The Right-Wing Backlash").

The Supreme Court decision suggested that no government should have the right to redistribute income in society. The three dissenting justices gave sharp opinions in the other direction. "Courts," Justice Harlan Stone remarked with angry satire, "are not the only agency of government that must be assumed to have capacity to govern."

In Iowa, the home of radical agricultural politics, the six majority justices were burned in effigy. There was little doubt generally that their judgment ran smack against farmers' wishes. In

referendums held in 1935 farmers had voted overwhelmingly—wheat farmers by 6 to 1, corn-hog producers by 8 to 1, and tobacco and cotton planters by 9 to 1—to continue the programs being offered under the AAA.

Grain Surplus

Oscar Heline, an Iowa farmer, recalled the problems caused by overproduction and how people tried to overcome them:

"Grain was being burned. It was cheaper than coal. Corn was being burned. A county just east of here, they burned corn in their courthouse all winter…. In South Dakota the county elevator listed corn as minus three cents…. If you wanted to sell 'em a bushel of corn, you had to bring in three cents. They couldn't afford to handle it…. People were determined to withhold produce from the market—livestock, cream, butter, eggs, what not. If they would dump the produce, they would force the market to a higher level. The farmers would man the highways and cream cans were emptied in ditches and eggs dumped out. They burned the trestle bridge, so that trains wouldn't be able to haul grain…. Something had to be done.

"The farmer is a pretty independent individual. He wants to be a conservative individual. He wants to be an honorable individual. He wants to pay his debts. But it was hard…."

A young girl in the corner of a kitchen in a tent home near Sallisaw, Sequoyah County, Oklahoma. Rural poverty was a serious problem during the Depression, particularly among tenant farmers and others who did not own the land they worked.

2. FARMING PROBLEMS

Economic problems were not the sole difficulty for farmers in the Depression years. Climatic conditions devastated them as well. Mechanization and erosion destroyed the viability of the land, as did wild temperature swings and weather patterns that created droughts and freezes.

OVERUSE OF THE LAND

Forests and soil were destroyed at a dangerously excessive rate. For decades conservationists had warned that overcultivation and deforestation would destroy the productivity of the land. On the prairies the semiarid flatlands had been stripped of protective grasses and planted with grain from horizon to horizon (see Chapter 3, "The Dust Bowl"). Farther west the rolling grassland of the open range had been stripped by grazing livestock. In the upland forests and woodlands of the South and East lumbering operations had left millions of acres of hillsides bare of the roots that locked soil in place and the organic matter that prevented rain running straight off into creeks and valleys.

EXTREME WEATHER

Bad weather made the situation worse. Drought in 1930 affected an area from Maryland and Virginia to Missouri and Arkansas, stretching south from the Great Lakes to the Gulf of Mexico. Twelve states recorded

record low rainfall that year. These drought conditions continued to spread in 1931. Although drought conditions are a normal part of climate change, this particular drought continued over a larger than normal area for a dangerously prolonged period. Maine and Vermont were the only states to escape drought between 1930 and 1936.

The severity of climatic conditions between 1934 and 1938 was like nothing Americans had experienced for generations. Extreme weather battered the land. Gripping winter cold was followed by drought and scorching summers. Floods, winds, hurricanes, and other natural disasters seemed relentless.

The cruelty of the climate seemed symbolic to many Americans of the bleak situation the country faced. The continuing economic problems seemed to threaten the very fabric of the American way of life. Elsewhere the values of capitalism and democracy had been eroded by communist revolution in the

Soviet Union, and by right-wing extremism in Germany and Japan (see Volume 6, Chapter 2, "The Victory of Authoritarianism").

RURAL POVERTY

The poorest of the poor in the farming community—the tenant farmers, sharecroppers, and farm laborers—were suspicious of government assistance and often too proud to accept any help other than an offer of a job. It became seemingly better for them to move to where there were jobs, rather than to continue to eke out an existence from nothing. Some of the tenant farmers had no

Southern Tenant Farmers Union

The effort to organize tenant farmers led to the creation of the Southern Tenant Farmers Union in 1934. The union, which echoed farmers' attempts at political organization in the 1890s, was called a "sort of a peasant uprising." Union officials fought to get government aid for their members and to stop evictions. Conservatives and land owners did not take kindly to union organizers, who were beaten and threatened. Such violence occurred throughout the South, and in Colorado, Arizona, and California— wherever organizers fought for the human dignity of their tenant farmers.

Members of the CCC plant trees on a bare hillside. Other CCC projects included soil conservation and flood control.

By 1942 more than two million young men had participated in the work program. At its peak more than 500 CCC camps could be found in national, state, and local parks.

NEW FARM RECOVERY ACT SOUGHT

The Supreme Court's challenge to the AAA meant that the government had to come up with another farm recovery bill to replace the earlier agency. The

choice. When the land owners received government subsidies for keeping their land fallow, they did not need people to work.

3. MORE RURAL REFORMS

The Roosevelt administration now turned its attention to two key issues in the countryside—the problem of irresponsible land use and the need for conservation programs to combat the damage being caused, and the problem of rural poverty.

THE CCC

One program born early in the Roosevelt era was the Civilian Conservation Corps (CCC), created by the Emergency Conservation Work Act in 1933 (see Volume 2, Chapter 5, "Putting People to Work"). This program was designed to put young men between the ages of 18 and 25 to work on a variety of projects—war veterans also joined the corps—including reforestation, road construction, soil

conservation, park construction, trail clearing, and flood control projects. It was estimated that CCC participants, often referred to as "enrollees," planted an estimated three billion trees during the program's existence from 1933 to 1942.

CCC Camps

Camps were active in all states. At one time Washington State alone had 14 camps. Under the auspices of the U.S. Bureau of Agricultural Engineering some 46 CCC camps worked solely on projects designed to shore up artificial drainage systems throughout the country on which farmers depended for irrigating crops.

In addition the CCCers assisted with cleaning up after natural disasters. During flooding of the Ohio River in 1937 the CCC camps in the area provided emergency aid. They also helped with disasters including the flooding of the Mississippi Valley and, in Vermont and New York, the blizzards and hurricanes of 1937.

Labor Day Hurricane

The CCC in the Florida Keys suffered a tragedy in 1935. Three CCC camps lay directly in the path of the Labor Day hurricane that struck Florida, said to have been one of the most violent storms on record. Fewer than a third of the 684 corpsmen were on vacation during the storm: The rest were in the camps, which were battered by winds of 150 to 200 miles per hour. A train sent from Miami to rescue camps occupants was derailed en route. CCC files recorded the devastation: "The official report listed 44 identified dead, 238 missing or unidentified dead, and 106 injured. Many were literally sandblasted to death, with clothing and skin rasped from their bodies."

new measure would need to make farmers eligible for government money without running foul of the Court. The matter was urgent, since 1936 was an election year, and Roosevelt wanted to maintain the goodwill of farmers who had benefited from the 1933 act.

A new law, the Soil Conservation and Domestic Allotment Act (1936), further reflected FDR's plan to bring agriculture under a form of national planning. It incurred the wrath of Republicans, who denounced it as intending only to keep "surplus" Democrats on the government's payroll. The new act, however, also highlighted an important new focus of agricultural policy, which was largely a result of the Dust Bowl conditions in the Midwest.

Soil Conservation and Domestic Allotment Act

The act established land and water conservation as national policy. It also provided for funding farmers for soil

and water-conservation activities. A resurrected version of a Soil Conservation Act of 1935, the new legislation was designed as a direct alternative to the now defunct AAA. The major differences between the two acts included the elimination of both the tax on processors and the benefits paid to farmers for taking their land out of production.

It was not the first New Deal measure to direct attention to the necessity of soil conservation. As early as October 1933 a Soil Erosion Service had been added to the Department of the Interior, and in 1934 Congress had passed a Grazing Act that brought grazing on lands in the public domain under national regulation. During the climate crises up to 4 inches (10 cm) of topsoil had blown away in some regions, making countless acres of farmland worthless. In 1935, as the continuing drought made a wasteland of much of the West, Congress authorized the establishment of a permanent Soil Conservation Service (SCS) within the Department of Agriculture to develop and implement a long-range conservation program. The 1936 act empowered the government to make bounty payments to

farmers who switched from growing soil-exhausting commercial crops like wheat and cotton to soil-nurturing grasses and legumes such as clover and soybean.

Conservation Methods

Projects aimed primarily to take endangered lands out of production or to plant pasturage or other crops that would not deplete the soil quality. Farmers were also taught about rotation crops. One plan on the devastated plains, where wheat was the traditional crop, called for a three-year rotation cycle: planting wheat followed by sorghum, and then allowing the land to remain fallow or unplanted the following year. Other techniques used to spare the land included counterplowing, terracing, and strip planting. In other areas farmers were shown how growing trees could shelter crops from harsh winds.

Publicizing Conservation Programs

In addition to the programs of agencies such as the Farm Security Administration (FSA) conservation work was carried out by other agencies, such as the Tennessee Valley Authority. The public was educated about these various efforts at agricultural planning by the films of Pare Lorenz. Created for the FSA, the documentaries *The Plow That Broke the Plains* and *The River* stimulated increased interest in conserving natural resources. This period between 1935 and 1940 was instrumental in beginning comprehensive national soil and water-conservation programs in the United States.

Alongside the Soil Conservation and Domestic Allotment Act President Roosevelt called on the

THE RAVAGES OF SOIL EROSION WITHIN 50 YEARS

Virgin

PRODUCTIVE SOIL 2/3 GONE

Eroded

A soil erosion poster designed to alert farmers to the fact that overuse of the soil had resulted in the erosion of two-thirds of the productive topsoil layer.

1930: A gully in the central Plains region, showing an advanced state of erosion. The dry, dusty soil, stripped of virtually all vegetation, has been blown away by wind.

country as a whole to wake up to the damage that was being done to the country's natural resources. The CCC enlisted almost three million men to help stem the degeneration of the environment. They planted 17 million acres of new forestland, built over six million small "check" dams to slow soil erosion, and initiated projects to reduce plant diseases. Over one-quarter of the nation's farmers took part in a program that involved building large dams and reservoirs and planting vast belts of trees to shelter the soil on the high plains.

Temporary Price-support Loans to Farmers
The Soil Conservation Act was a thinly veiled attempt to get around the Supreme Court ruling

and continue the policy of payments to farmers for reduced crop production. However, without the taxing power and the direct benefits given to farmers who lost employment under the original act, the new legislation was inadequate for its purpose. So long as the drought continued, the shortcomings in the legislation hardly mattered, since dry summers continued to have the effect of controlling production. However, when the drought ended in the summer of 1937, and it became apparent that record crops would be harvested, Congress approved temporary price-support loans to farmers. The next year a second major farm act was passed to fill the void created by the Supreme Court.

THE SECOND AAA
The second Agricultural Adjustment Administration, enacted in 1938, supplanted the Soil Conservation and Domestic Allotment Act of 1936. This

1934: The same gully, transformed by the Soil Conservation Service with fast-growing plants that anchor the soil and prevent it from being swept away.

legislation contained some features from the original AAA, but also included a step further in national agricultural planning with the "ever-normal granary." Devised by Secretary of Agriculture Henry Wallace, the idea involved banking surplus grain until times of need. A food-stamp program gave the urban poor access to the food supplies.

The 1938 act was the last substantial piece of New Deal legislation for agriculture. It dressed in altered clothing the old principles of controlled production and price-support loans. Production was to be curtailed on a voluntary basis by acreage allotments. Compulsory controls were to be imposed only when supplies became excessive, and then only if two-thirds of farmers agreed to

A group of farmers at a soil conservation meeting in Livingston County, Illinois, 1937. Roosevelt's government encouraged farmers to become involved in making decisions about farming issues.

Flaws in the New AAA

The provisions of the act were so complicated and working out quotas so time-consuming that many farmers were left feeling bewildered. In this as in other ways the AAA favored large-scale commerical farming—now called agribusiness—which could more easily plan its output. Decisions were made so late in the year that growers had to send their crops to market before knowing what quotas would be placed on them.

In the midterm elections of November 1938 Democratic

them in a referendum. If the farmers voted in favor of compulsory sales, quotas would be set, and those farmers who failed to keep within them would have their excess sales heavily taxed.

Referendums

The use of referendums, in which the electorate vote on a single issue, was one of the most remarkable aspects of the New Deal. Since the late 19th century the Progressive movement had put referendums high on its agenda for creating a more democratic society. Roosevelt was the first president to make systematic use of them. Millions of farmers—among them many black farmers who had never participated in any form of balloting before—voted on issues that directly affected them in the 1930s, such as the creation of soil conservation areas. Nor were referendums Roosevelt's only nod in the direction of direct democracy. More than 100,000 representatives of the agricultural economy served on the committees the AAA used to implement its farming policies, and the Grazing Act of 1934 laid down that decisions to cordon off public grasslands on which grazing was not to be permitted had to be made in cooperation with livestock producers.

That the government relied so heavily on such mechanisms to ensure that it carried the farming population along with it testified to the groundbreaking nature of its farm policy. To break so sharply with the dominant philosophy of the 1920s—that government should intervene as minimally as possible in the economy—was a radical solution to a desperate situation. To make the break first in agriculture, the most conservative sector of the economy, was to risk massive resistance. If the adventure were to succeed, it was clear that policies could not simply be imposed on the farmers by Washington officials. Crop control, as originally laid down by the AAA, was to be voluntary. Farmers could not be forced to sign contracts with the AAA. Their cooperation was essential, not merely to make the program operable, but to convince Congress, especially those members from farming states, that it had the backing of the people who elected them.

candidates felt the force of smaller farmers' irritation with the act. The Republicans made substantial gains in the Midwest. In a referendum held in December tobacco growers, who had voted in favor of compulsory controls nine months earlier, voted against setting them for the following year.

Appointment of Local Committees

There was a further consideration. Among the staple products of the agricultural economy only milk and cattle had their own producer organizations capable of implementing a policy that would require thousands of people to administer and monitor. The provision by the AAA for the appointment of local committees to manage the government's schemes contained an element of "grass-roots" democracy. The committees that were appointed came in for the criticism that they were composed of wealthy landowners who did not have the interests of sharecroppers and tenant farmers at heart. Supporters of the committees argued that it was natural that men of influence in their local communities should be those who came to the attention of AAA officials. In any case, they maintained, small farmers had no time to sit on boards and committees, and agricultural laborers rarely had the expertise or confidence to be of much influence.

Despite such criticisms, the AAA was remarkably effective in swinging farming opinion behind the government. In the first year of the new AAA the readiness of farmers to sign crop-control contracts was beyond expectations. Over three-quarters of cotton fields were brought under contract, over 90 percent of Iowa's corn fields, and nearly all of South Dakota's. Nine out of ten tobacco farmers also came into line.

THE RESETTLEMENT ADMINISTRATION

Among the first legislation enacted in 1933 to alleviate housing problems in rural communities across the country was the Emergency Farm Mortgage Act, which was designed to protect farms from foreclosure. The Supreme Court challenged legislation aimed at preventing

The corner of a bedroom on a farm near Milford, Iowa, 1936. The impoverished occupants received aid from the RA.

One of the Penderlea homesteads in North Carolina, 1936. Under the New Deal these homesteads were built to house poor urban and farming families.

foreclosures. Starting in 1935, under the Subsistence Homestead Division of the Interior Department of the Resettlement Administration (RA), the federal government started a series of programs to provide for people who traditionally made their living from the land, but who, because of unwise land use or drought, had fallen on hard times.

The main goal of the RA was to provide poor farm families with the means to buy land and start their own farms. The program was designed to provide these families with education on many topics critical to their independence and success, including agricultural

Workers in a vacuum cleaner factory at Reedsville, West Virginia, 1937. Many of the employees were homesteaders from Arthurdale.

methods, nutrition, and finance. In some places where the earth had been exhausted by overuse, people were relocated wholesale—either to new farms or to one of the suburbs that had started appearing across the country.

Led by agrarian reformer and undersecretary of agriculture Rexford Tugwell (see box, opposite) the RA was responsible for a

variety of projects. They included running produce markets in New Orleans and constructing planned communities.

Cooperative Communities for Displaced Farmers

When the RA moved farmers off poor or submarginal land, some entire neighborhoods were relocated. The idea was that people

Rexford Tugwell

Born in Sinclairville, New York, Rexford Guy Tugwell (1891–1979) moved to Wilson, New York, in 1904. After graduating from high school, he went on to study and, later, teach economics. By 1932 Tugwell had been made a professor at Columbia University. His interest in and knowledge of agriculture led to his recruitment into Roosevelt's Brain Trust in 1932, and in 1933 he was made assistant secretary of agriculture. That same year he coauthored the Agricultural Adjustment Act. He became undersecretary of agriculture in 1934.

During 1933 and 1934 Tugwell devoted his energy to promoting soil conservation; in the 1936 drought he reported that he had visited "every center of our vast organization to see that everything possible was done."

Tugwell (right) speaks to a Dust Bowl farmer in the Texas panhandle in 1936.

In 1935 Tugwell was appointed head of the Resettlement Administration. He helped evicted tenant farmers and sharecroppers, and campaigned on behalf of the poor and the blacks. Criticism of his "socialist" influences led to his being forced out of the Department of Agriculture in 1937.

could be moved to areas where the soil was in better condition, and where they would have better employment opportunities, while experts would work to restore the overworked soil to some form of usefulness. An estimated 10 million acres of exhausted land were allowed to lie fallow.

The families were moved into experimental cooperative communities, described by one critic as "a mixture of Karl Marx and nineteenth-century utopianism, with a subsidy from the national treasury." These communities, like Penderlea Homesteads in North Carolina and Jersey Homesteads in New Jersey, included numerous small farms built in an area with

•

"…a mixture of Karl Marx and nineteenth-century utopianism…"

•

government assistance. The relocated farmers were encouraged to establish cooperatives for such tasks as equipment purchases and marketing goods. For many Americans the ideas behind such communities seemed uncomfortably close to socialism or communism.

Subsistence Farming Communities
A few areas were formed as experimental subsistence farming communities. They combined small three-to-five-acre farms with other businesses that supported

Greenbelt, Maryland

Greenbelt, Maryland, was the first of three model communities constructed by the Resettlement Administration "to demonstrate that good homes in lovely surroundings can be within reach of city families with only moderate incomes." Although numerous other communities had been planned, only two other towns were ever completed: Greendale, Wisconsin, and Greenhills, Ohio.

Greenbelt thrived and today remains a lively community. It was named for the belt of woodland surrounding it and the green belts

Neat row houses line an approach road to Greenbelt, photographed in 1941. The sign promotes the community's role in providing homes for defense workers.

between neighborhoods that provided close proximity to nature. As explained in a city history, it was "designed as a complete city, with businesses, schools, roads, and facilities for recreation and town government." In addition, it boasted "one of the first mall-type shopping centers in the United States."

One account described Greenbelt as an experiment in both physical and social planning. The two major streets were curved and ran along the top and bottom of a crescent-shaped natural ridge. In the center of the crescent stood the stores, the school, ball fields, and various community buildings. Around this center stood homes arranged in "superblocks." Walkways allowed residents to go from home to town center without crossing a major street. Vehicular traffic was carefully kept away from areas where people walked. The architecture was streamlined Art Deco, and federally sponsored artists contributed to this theme with sculptures.

A cooperative store at Greenbelt, Maryland, 1938. Other cooperative services at Greenbelt included a gas station, movie theater, barbershop, drugstore, and a beauty parlor.

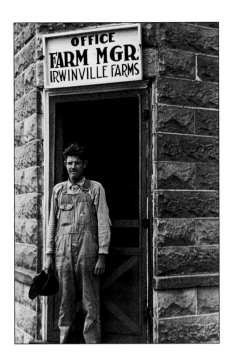

A farmer reports to the manager's office at Irwinville Farms, an RA project in California, in May 1938. The RA loaned money to farmers and organized cooperatives.

Agricultural land surrounded a residential tract in which planned, affordable housing was available. Greenbelt communities were also designed to accommodate cars, with wide roads and ample parking.

In reality the towns were more suited to dealing with urban degeneration than rural poverty, which was too deep-rooted to be tackled by resettlement projects. At any rate, the RA received only a small amount of money from a Congress suspicious of anything that resembled socialism. Tugwell had started with high hopes of moving around 500,000 families.

In the end the program moved just under 4,500.

In all, the New Deal's rural housing and community program actually created only about 8,000 housing units in 96 rural communities, ranging in size from 11 to 294 units. The program, which began life under the Subsistence Homestead Division of the Interior Department, was transfered to the RA in 1935 and finally to the Farm Security Administration (FSA), under which it remained until after World War II.

THE FARM SECURITY ADMINISTRATION

More far-reaching in its intended effect was a bill introduced in the Senate by William Bankhead (1874–1940) to help tenant farmers and farm laborers acquire land for themselves. Between

the farmers, primarily craft workshops and light manufacturing firms. First Lady Eleanor Roosevelt was a huge proponent of this program; she all but launched the program herself in a community called Arthurdale, in the depressed coal-mining region of West Virginia.

Greenbelt Towns

The agency also built three experimental suburban communities, known as greenbelt town projects, of the kind that had been pioneered in England, where they were called "garden cities." Located in greenbelt areas near large towns that could offer employment, such as Washington, D.C. and Milwaukee, Wisconsin, these planned communities were intended to accommodate agricultural use in a greenbelt.

A father relaxing with his daughter after a day spent working in the pea fields, 1939. They were staying in an FSA migratory labor camp at Brawley, California. The tent platform they are sitting on was standard equipment in FSA camps.

Rural Electrification Administration

In 1935 President Roosevelt established the Rural Electrification Administration (REA), a government plan to bring electricity to rural areas. In so doing he hoped to raise living standards in rural areas and to slow the widespread migration of Americans from the countryside to the towns and cities.

At that time only one farm in ten was supplied with electricity. In the poorest states of the south, like Mississippi, the figure was nearer one in 100. In 1933 the majority of farms relied on gasoline engines, manual labor, and animal power. Not only did the lack of electrical power prevent farmers from modernizing their farms and reducing the labor costs of farming; it also condemned families to dingy, inadequately heated homes and poor sanitation, thus contributing to poor health. Nine out of ten farms had no running water, and inhabitants had to fetch water from nearby streams or draw it from wells. America was increasingly divided into two nations: the electrified city dwellers and rural households still in the dark age.

Privately owned utility companies kept out of rural areas because the costs of supplying electricity to small populations scattered over large areas was unprofitable. During the 1920s alternative solutions were tried, including the formation of cooperatives. Cooperatives were often poorly managed, however, and suffered from a lack of technical and financial expertise.

A strong advocate of rural electrification—he believed that public power should be shared by all, not hoarded by a privileged few—engineer Morris Cooke worked with Roosevelt and the government to draw up a plan for rural electrification. The result was the creation of the REA in May 1935, with Cooke as its first administrator.

An REA Cooperative in Rush County. The REA made low-cost loans to nonprofit electrical cooperatives set up by farmers. As a result, the number of farms with an electricity supply increased from 750,000 in 1935 to 2.3 million in 1941.

With private companies still unwilling to take part in a rural electrification program, Cooke turned instead to nonprofit-making cooperatives set up by the farmers themselves. Against the opposition of the private companies, he granted cooperatives preference for REA loans by which they could acquire the necessary generating and distributing facilities to supply their farms with electric power. Thus the cooperatives were able to construct power lines and bring electricity into areas not served by private companies. In areas that

A farmer's wife in Georgia stocks her new electric refrigerator in 1938. Electricity brought the conveniences of urban living to the countryside.

also made possible the automation of certain operations, saving labor and helping increase productivity.

The introduction of electrification into the countryside did help narrow the gap between urban and rural life, but it did not itself stall the flow of farmworkers to the cities, which carried on. In fact, electrification actually led to a greater use of automation and mechanization on the farms and thus reduced the need for manual labor, creating more rural unemployment. Nevertheless, the REA remains one of the great successes of the FDR administration, since it achieved the key objective set for it by the New Deal— to provide low-cost electricity to the rural areas of America.

were already serviced by private electricity companies, REA cooperatives were able to purchase their power at wholesale rates and distribute it to their members.

In districts that took advantage of the REA loans it was a moment of great excitement when neighbors gathered on hilltops to await the switching on of their generator for the first time and to see their homes flooded with light. By 1941, 40 percent of American farms had electricity. By 1950 the figure had rise to 90 percent.

The effects of electrification were felt everywhere. For women in particular, electric refrigerators, stoves, and vacuum cleaners provided at least a partial escape from the drudgery of housekeeping chores. The whole family enjoyed the pleasures to be got from radios, record players, and improved lighting. On the farm itself electricity

A linesman for an REA cooperative at work in Hayti, Missouri. The construction and maintenance of electricity transmission lines provided more jobs, thereby stimulating the economy.

1930 and 1935 the number of tenant farmers across the nation had increased by 200,000, a statistic alarming to people who remained inspired by the old Jeffersonian ideal of a property-owning democracy. The Bankhead-Jones Farm Tenancy Act became law in 1937. It provided for the establishment of a Farm Security Administration to replace the RA.

Unlike previous versions of rural housing programs, when the FSA was formed in 1937, agency officials worked to keep smaller farmers on their land. Of America's 6.5 million farms, over half were under 100 acres in size and generally too small to support a family. Although the government favored large agribusinesses, it needed to keep farmers' votes by at least providing aid for them. The FSA provided long-term, low-interest loans to these farmers to either enlarge their holdings or—in the case of tenant farmers and

sharecroppers—to purchase their own land.

Administered by the Department of Agriculture, the FSA's programs had formerly come under the jurisdiction of the Federal Emergency Relief Administration. The FSA, essentially the social service section of the AAA, was highly controversial. It was at odds with agencies that worked mainly on behalf of farmers with large holdings, and Congress offered it little financial support. Tugwell, one of the president's closest advisers as well as the head of the RA, quit the agency in 1937. His resignation weakened the effectiveness of the agency.

By the end of 1941 the FSA, which also managed camps for migrant workers, had spent nearly $1 billion, mostly on loans for farm purchase. It had also introduced a number of innovative projects, such as medical-care cooperatives, and had made loans to cooperatives of wheat farmers to enable

Men, women, and children work on an FSA cooperative in Louisiana in August 1940. The FSA helped poor farmers organize but lacked funds to really tackle rural poverty.

them to buy grain elevators, thus cutting out one intermediary between them and the market.

The FSA, though it existed for a shorter time than the AAA, achieved comparable results in terms of its effect on individuals. Through 1940 it continued to make short-term rehabilitation loans averaging $500 per borrower. Longer-term loans were available for tenant farmers to puchase their own land.

The FSA drew praise from liberals for its equal treatment of whites and blacks, but the people it was trying to help—inarticulate, disorganized farm laborers and tenants—did not have the political clout to get enough funding for FSA programs to make a real dent in rural poverty. In the end only the prosperity brought by World War II produced a fall in the number of tenant farms. In 1935 two-fifths of the nation's farms were held in tenancy, and in eight southern states, over half. By 1950 the national figure had dropped to one-quarter, and only in one southern state, Mississippi, was the figure still above one-half.

FSA programs were criticized by other governmental agencies whose programs were primarily designed to help larger agricultural interests, as well as by groups supporting agricultural special interests. Roosevelt came under attack in 1939 and 1940 primarily from the American Farm Bureau Federation. The condemnation was inspired not only by the government programs but also by frustration at the weakening political clout of the farm bureaus.

Demise of the FSA

The FSA had many political enemies. Among the faults of which it was regularly accused were extravagance, unwise investments, and "coddling" its clients. Some critics accused it of being un-American for its echoes of socialism. The critics got their way. In 1938 Congress directed the FSA to liquidate its resettlement projects and to start no new ones. After that its budget was progressively cut back, and its activities waned. In 1944 it was closed down. Continued lobbying efforts would successfully weaken or terminate all the rest of the various New Deal agricultural aid programs as World War II approached.

Surplus commodities on sale at a store in 1936. Purchases could be made using the government-issued food stamps, designed to encourage people to buy farm products.

4. RESULTS OF NEW DEAL AGRICULTURAL POLICY

Great time and effort were spent on the attempt to sustain the agricultural economy. How successful were the results? Critics at the time and since have presented a compelling argument that the New Deal accomplished little. Their argument is that the stop-gap methods used, principally crop-control and price-support mechanisms, left no time for a long-term solution to farming's problems. In addition, they argue that planned scarcity, which is what Wallace and Roosevelt sought to achieve, was wasteful and immoral in a nation in which millions were hungry and ill-clothed. The real problem was not overproduction but under-consumption and inadequate distribution. Finally, critics point out that production was cut not so much (if at all) by the AAA's programs as by the long drought of 1933 to 1936. Perhaps as much as 95 percent of the reduction in the wheat crop, for example, was caused by drought. Once good weather and the war economy came to farming's rescue, surpluses piled up once more.

SHORT-TERM SOLUTION TO AGRICULTURAL RECOVERY

Supporters of the New Deal answered those charges by saying that it was never the intention to come up with long-term solutions. No more than anyone else did they enjoy burning crops and destroying pigs. However, the sharp onset of the Depression required an immediate response, a short-term solution. A profitable agricultural economy was essential as the basis for general economic recovery. If the farmers had no money to buy industrial goods, manufacturing industry would remain in a slump.

With the benefit of hindsight some observers now believe that New Dealers focused too narrowly on the immediate difficulties

Eleanor Roosevelt plants a tree at a Girl Scout clubhouse in Washington, D.C., in 1937. Tree planting was heavily encouraged as a method of soil conservation and as a way to improve the natural beauty of the United States.

demand as the key to economic recovery remains a debatable question. What of the larger picture? On a number of fronts bolder action might have been taken. Agricultural prices might have been kept down by government subsidies to farmers. An attempt to reform the framework of food-processing and distribution might have been made. More might have been done to get food surpluses into the kitchens of the poor and to

get more land into the ownership of small farmers. More, too, might have been done to relieve the poverty of workers on Southern plantations and factory farms in California. Raising prices temporarily raised the incomes of ordinary people on the family farms of the Midwest. It did little for the dispossessed workers on cotton plantations, where the owners kept most of the increased profits for themselves. The reforms needed to eliminate all rural poverty would have amounted to the complete overthrow of the traditional agricultural system; Roosevelt's government had neither the mandate nor the will to do this.

Whether, as some critics have suggested, the New Deal would have done better by keeping more tenants and small farmers working

facing the nation in a time of financial depression. Soil conservation provides a case in point. The efforts of the Soil Conservation Service to salvage the lands of the Great Plains were successful if measured purely by the speed with which the land was returned to cultivation. From a longer perspective, however, what was accomplished in the 1930s merely enabled farmers to overgrow wheat again. Dust storms returned in the 1950s and the 1970s. Farmers could have been educated to exploit the land less ruthlessly.

MORE RADICAL ALTERNATIVES
Whether the Roosevelt government was right to fix its attention on rural rather than urban

Large-scale agriculture on a ranch in the Imperial Valley, California, 1939. This type of farming, favored by New Deal policies, was responsible for displacing many of the smaller farmers and also for damaging the soil.

the land is questionable. It was beyond the imagination in the 1930s to foresee the dramatic transformation of American agriculture that was to take place after 1945 as banks and rich corporations funded the growth of agribusiness. That change drove farmers off the land in their thousands. All societies have found that as they become more industrialized, they require a smaller percentage of the workforce to be engaged in farming. The New Deal's aim was to alleviate distress in the 1930s, not to stop the march of history.

APPORTIONING BLAME

Some historians assert that big business should take the blame for precipitating the developments that ultimately caused the demise of small farmers. Already in 1942 one author was describing farmers as "the victims of grab and greed as much as dust and tractors."

This farm in Oneida County, Idaho, was purchased by the Resettlement Administration in 1936, after the farmer's efforts to raise crops on poor, submarginal land had failed. The RA bought such farms to restore them to grazing land.

Countryside & Small Stock Journal, in an assessment of farmers' behavior, concluded that "The goal was immediate personal gain. The rationale was the building of a great nation on democratic and capitalistic principles. The result was destroyed land and lives. Few could protest. Most were convinced that the soil could never be destroyed. The water could never run out…. The forests were only important as timber, not as ecological systems. The exploitation of the land was building great

•

"…the victims of grab and greed as much as dust and tractors."

•

cities, a great culture, great wealth. This was The American Way."

The sum effect of aid to farmers was to make the federal government far more important in agriculture than before. Federal measures concentrated, however,

on those farmers impoverished by the Depression. They did not attempt to address the problem of rural poverty or the plight of rural Americans who had lived below the poverty line before the Depression. In its more limited goal the administration could reasonably claim success. Farmers' incomes doubled from 1932 to the end of the decade.

A more significant statistic, however, was that the rural population fell by over a fifth during the decade. Bad weather, low product prices, and the spread of larger farms had driven many farmers in the Midwest to head either west to California or into towns. By the end of the decade approximately 60 percent of the population was living in urban centers.

GLOSSARY

balanced budget an economic term used to describe a situation in which a government's income is enough to pay for all its expenditure. The balanced budget was an essential principle in U.S. economic policy until Roosevelt adopted deficit spending in 1937. *See also* deficit spending.

business cycle an economic term used to describe the periodic but unpredictable and inexplicable rise and fall of economic activity.

capitalism an economic system in which private individuals and companies control the production and distribution of goods and services.

communism a political doctrine advocated by Karl Marx and Friedrich Engels in the 19th century that proposes the overthrow of capitalism and its replacement by working-class rule. Communism was the official ideology of the Soviet Union and was highly feared in the United States.

deficit spending an economic approach in which a government goes into debt in order to fund its activities. Deficit spending is a central tenet of Keynesianism.

depression a deep trough in the business cycle. No other depression matched the intensity of or lasted as long as the Great Depression.

fascism a political ideology based on authoritarian rule and suppression, aggressive nationalism, and militarism.

gold standard an economic tool that used gold as the measure of a nation's currency, so that one unit of currency always bought a fixed amount of gold. It was chiefly useful in stabilizing exchange rates between currencies.

Hundred Days the name given to Roosevelt's first period as president, from March 9 to June 16, 1933, characterized by a whirl of legislative activity. It was named for the Hundred Days of the 19th-century French emperor Napoleon.

individualism a political philosophy that argues that individuals are most effective when they are responsible only for their own well-being and not for that of other members of society.

installment buying a method of buying originally introduced by car companies in the 1920s that allowed purchasers to make a downpayment on a purchase and then pay the balance in a series of regular installments.

isolationism an approach adopted in the United States after World War I that argued that the country should disassociate itself from affairs elsewhere in the world. It led to the U.S. failure to join the League of Nations.

Keynesianism the economic theory advocated by John Maynard Keynes in the 1920s and 1930s. Keynes argued that governments should spend money to maintain full employment and stimulate the economy. His theories dominated most western democracies from the 1930s to around the 1980s.

labor union a formal organization in which workers act collectively in order to protect their interests such as pay and work conditions.

laissez-faire a French term for "let it be," used to describe an economy with no government regulation of business activity. Laissez-faire is an important part of classical or free-market economics, which holds that laws of supply and demand alone should regulate prices, wages, and other economic factors.

liberalism a political theory that emphasizes a belief in progress, the autonomy of individuals, and the protection of political and civil rights; also an economic theory based on competition and the free market.

mixed economy an economy that combines characteristics of a free-market economy—competition, private ownership—with a limited amount of state involvement, such as regulation of business, wage and hour legislation, and a degree of nationalization.

mutualism a U.S. political tradition that advocates cooperative action as a way to lessen the negative social effects of the economy. The mutualist tradition was behind the general acceptance in the 1930s that government had an obligation to look after its citizens.

nativism an anti-immigrant U.S. political tradition that values "real" Americans and their attitudes over those of more recent immigrants. In the late 19th century nativism saw first- or second-generation Irish immigrants objecting to newcomers from southern Europe, for example.

planned economy an economy in which economic activity is controlled by the state. Most businesses are nationalized rather than privately owned, and the government sets production quotas, wages, and prices.

populism a name given to numerous political movements of the 1930s that claimed to represent the common people; populism also describes the beliefs of the Populist Party formed in 1891 to represent rural interests and the breakup of monopolies.

progressivism a political tradition in the United States that advocated social reform by government legislation. Both the Republican and Democratic parties had progressive wings.

public works projects often large-scale projects run by federal, state, or local government in order to generate employment.

recession a severe decline in economic activity that lasts for at least six months

regulation a word used to describe moves by government or other agencies to control business activity, such as by legislation relating to minimum wages or maximum working hours or health and safety procedures.

relief the term most often used in the 1920s and 1930s for welfare.

Social Darwinism a social theory based on the theory of natural selection proposed by Charles Darwin. Social Darwinists believed that some people inevitably became richer or more powerful than others, and that inequality was therefore acceptable.

socialism a political doctrine that removes business from private owner-ship in favor of state or cooperative ownership in order to create a more equitable society.

welfare financial or other help distributed to people in need; the word is also sometimes used to apply to the agencies that distribute the aid.

FURTHER READING

Allen, Frederick Lewis. *Since Yesterday: The 1930s in America, September 3, 1929–September 3, 1939.* New York: HarperCollins, 1986.

Brogan, Hugh. *The Penguin History of the United States of America.* New York: Penguin Books, 1990.

Evans, Harold. *The American Century.* New York: Knopf, 1999.

Handlin, Oscar, and Lilian Handlin. *Liberty and Equality: 1920–1994.* New York: HarperCollins Publishers, 1994.

Jones, M. A. *The Limits of Liberty: American History 1607–1992.* New York: Oxford University Press, 1995.

Kennedy, David M. *Freedom From Fear: The American People in Depression and War, 1929–1945* (Oxford History of the United States). New York: Oxford University Press, 1999.

Meltzer, Milton. *Brother Can You Spare a Dime?: The Great Depression 1929–1933* New York: Facts on File, Inc., 1991.

Nardo, Don (ed.). *The Great Depression* (Opposing Viewpoints Digest). Greenhaven Press, 1998.

Parrish, Michael E. *Anxious Decades: America in Prosperity and Depression, 1920–1941.* New York: W. W. Norton & Company Inc., 1994.

Phillips, Cabell. *From the Crash to the Blitz: 1929-1939.* Bronx, NY: Fordham University Press, 2000.

Watkins, T. H. *The Great Depression: America in the 1930s.* Boston: Little Brown and Co, 1995.

Worster, Donald. *Dust Bowl: The Southern Plains in the 1930s.* New York: Oxford University Press, 1982

NOVELS AND EYEWITNESS ACCOUNTS

Agee, James, and Walker Evans. *Let Us Now Praise Famous Men.* Boston: Houghton Mifflin Co., 2000

Burg, David F. *The Great Depression: An Eyewitness History.* New York: Facts on File, Inc., 1996

Caldwell, Erskine. *God's Little Acre.* Athens, GA: University of Georgia Press, 1995.

Caldwell, Erskine, and Margaret Bourke-White. *You Have Seen Their Faces.* Athens, GA: University of Georgia Press, 1995.

Dos Passos, John. *U.S.A.* New York: Library of America, 1996.

Farell, James T. *Studs Lonigan: A Trilogy.* Urbana: University of Illinois Press, 1993.

Faulkner, William. *Absalom, Absalom!* Boston: McGraw Hill College Division, 1972.

Hemingway, Ernest. *To Have and Have Not.* New York: Scribner, 1996.

———. *For Whom the Bell Tolls.* New York: Scribner, 1995.

Le Sueur, Meridel. *Salute to Spring.* New York: International Publishers Co., Inc., 1977.

McElvaine, Robert S. *Down and Out in the Great Depression: Letters from the Forgotten Man.* Chapel Hill, NC: University of North Carolina Press, 1983.

Olsen, Tillie. *Yonnondio: From the Thirties.* New York: Delta, 1979.

Smedley, Agnes. *Daughter of Earth: A Novel.* New York: Feminist Press, 1987.

Steinbeck, John. *The Grapes of Wrath.* New York: Penguin USA, 1992.

———. *Of Mice and Men.* New York: Penguin USA, 1993.

Terkel, Studs. *Hard Times: An Oral History of the Great Depression.* New York: The New Press, 2000.

Wright, Richard. *Native Son.* New York: HarperCollins, 1989.

PROLOGUE TO THE DEPRESSION

Allen, Frederick Lewis. *Only Yesterday.* New York: Harper and Brothers, 1931.

Bordo, Michael D., Claudia Goldin, and Eugene N. White (eds.). *The Defining Moment: The Great Depression and the American Economy in the Twentieth Century.* Chicago: University of Chicago Press, 1998.

Cohen, Lizabeth. *Making a New Deal.* New York: Cambridge University Press, 1990.

Galbraith, John Kenneth. *The Great Crash 1929.* Boston: Houghton Mifflin Co., 1997.

Kennedy, David M. *Over Here: The First World War and American Society.* New York: Oxford University Press, 1980.

Knock, T. J. *To End All Wars: Woodrow Wilson and the Quest for a New World Order.* Princeton, NJ: Princeton University Press.

Levian, J. R. *Anatomy of a Crash, 1929.* Burlington, VT: Fraser Publishing Co., 1997.

Sobel, Robert. *The Great Bull Market: Wall Street in the 1920s.* New York: W. W. Norton & Company Inc., 1968.

———. *Panic on Wall Street.* New York: Macmillan, 1968.

Wilson, Joan Hoff. *Herbert Hoover: Forgotten Progressive.* Boston: Little, Brown, 1975.

FDR AND OTHER INDIVIDUALS

Alsop, Joseph. *FDR: 1882–1945.* New York: Gramercy, 1998.

Brinkley, Alan. *Voices of Protest: Huey Long, Father Coughlin, and the Great Depression.* New York: Knopf, 1982.

Cook, Blanche Wiesen. *Eleanor Roosevelt: A Life.* New York: Viking, 1992.

Fried, Albert, *FDR and His Enemies.* New York: St. Martin's Press, 1999.

Graham, Otis L., Jr., and Meghan Wander (eds.) *Franklin D. Roosevelt, His Life and Times: An Encyclopedic View.* Boston: G.K. Hall & Co, 1985.

Hunt, John Gabriel, and Greg Suriano (eds.). *The Essential Franklin Delano Roosevelt: FDR's Greatest Speeches, Fireside Chats, Messages, and Proclamations.* New York: Gramercy, 1998.

Maney, Patrick J. *The Roosevelt Presence: The Life and Legacy of FDR.* Berkeley: University of California Press, 1998.

Roosevelt, Eleanor. *The Autobiography of Eleanor Roosevelt.* New York: Da Capo Press, 2000.

Watkins, T. H. *Righteous Pilgrim: The Life and Times of Harold L. Ickes.* New York: Henry Holt, 1990.

White, Graham. *Harold Ickes of the New Deal: His Private Life and Public Career.* Cambridge, MA: Harvard University Press, 1985.

SOCIAL HISTORY

Clausen, John A. *American Lives: Looking Back at the Children of the Great Depression.* Berkeley, CA: University of California Press, 1995.

Elder, Glen H., Jr. *Children of the Great Depression.* New York: HarperCollins, 1998.

Gregory, James N. *American Exodus: The Dust Bowl Migration and Okie Culture in California.* New York: Oxford University Press, 1991.

Katz, Michael B. *In the Shadow of the Poorhouse: A Social History of Welfare in America.* New York: Basic Books, 1997.

Lowitt, Richard, and Maurine Beasley (eds.). *One Third of a Nation: Lorena Hickok Reports on the Great Depression.* Urbana: University of Illinois Press, 1981.

McGovern, James R. *And a Time for Hope: Americans and the Great Depression.* Westport, CT: Praeger Publishers, 2000.

Patterson, James T. *America's Struggle Against Poverty: 1900–1980.* Cambridge, MA: Harvard University Press, 1981.

Starr, Kevin. *Endangered Dreams: The Great Depression in California* (Americans and the California Dream). New York: Oxford University Press, 1996.

Ware, Susan. *Holding the Line: American Women in the 1930s.* Boston: Twayne, 1982.

Weiss, Nancy. *Farewell to the Party of Lincoln: Black Politics in the Age of FDR.* Princeton: Princeton University Press, 1983.

CULTURE AND THE ARTS

Benet's Reader's Encyclopedia of American Literature. New York: Harpercollins, 1996.

Davidson, Abraham A. *Early American Modernist Painting, 1910–1935.* New York: Da Capo Press, 1994.

Haskell, Barbara. *The American Century: Art & Culture, 1900–1950.* New York: W. W. Norton & Co., 1999.

Hughes, Robert. *American Visions: The Epic History of Art in America.* New York: Knopf, 1999.

McJimsey, George. *Harry Hopkins: Ally of the Poor and Defender of Democracy.* Cambridge, Mass.: Harvard University Press, 1987.

Meltzer, Milton. *Violins and Shovels: The WPA Arts Projects.* New York: Delacorte Press, 1976.

———. *Dorothea Lange: A Photographer's Life.* Syracuse, NY: Syracuse University Press, 2000.

Pells, R. H. *Radical Visions and American Dreams: Culture and Social Thought in the Depression Years.* Urbana: Illinios University Press, 1998.

Pollack, Howard. *Aaron Copland: The Life and Work of an Uncommon Man.* New York: Henry Holt & Co., Inc., 1999.

Thomson, David. *Rosebud: The Story of Orson Welles.* New York: Vintage Books, 1997.

Wilson, Edmond. *The American Earthquake: A Document of the 1920s and 1930s.* Garden City, NY: Doubleday, 1958.

INTERNATIONAL AFFAIRS

Bullock, Alan. *Hitler: A Study in Tyranny.* New York: Harper and Row, 1962.

Dallek, Robert. *Franklin D. Roosevelt and American Foreign Policy.* New York: Oxford University Press, 1979.

Kindleberger, Charles P. *The World in Depression, 1929–1939.* Berkeley: University of California Press, 1986.

Offner, A. A. *The Origins of the Second World War: American Foreign Policy and World Politics.* Melbourne, FL: Krieger Publishing Company, 1986.

Pauley, B. F. *Hitler, Stalin, and Mussolini: Totalitarianism in the Twentieth Century.* Wheeling, IL: Harlan Davidson, 1997.

Ridley, J. *Mussolini.* New York: St. Martin's Press, 1998.

WEB SITES

African American Odyssey: The Depression, The New Deal, and World War II
http://lcweb2.loc.gov/ammem/aaohtml/exhibit/aopart8.html

America from the Great Depression to World War II: Photographs from the FSA and OWI, 1935–1945

http://memory.loc.gov/ammem/fsowhome.html

The American Experience: Surviving the Dust Bowl
http://www.pbs.org/wgbh/amex/dustbowl

Biographical Directory of the United States Congress
http://bioguide.congress.gov

By the People, For the People: Posters from the WPA, 1936–1943
http://memory.loc.gov/ammem/wpaposters/wpahome.html

Federal Theater Project
http://memory.loc.gov/ammem/fedtp/fthome.html

Huey Long
http://www.lib.lsu.edu/special/long.html

The New Deal Network, Franklin and Eleanor Roosevelt Institute
http://newdeal.feri.org

New York Times Archives
http://www.nytimes.com

Presidents of the United States
http://www.ipl.org/ref/POTUS.html

The Scottsboro Boys
http://www.english.upenn.edu/~afilreis/88/scottsboro.html

Voices from the Dust Bowl: The Charles L. Todd and Robert Sonkin Migrant Worker Collection, 1940–1941
http://memory.loc.gov/ammem/afctshtml/tshome.html

WPA American Life Histories
http://lcweb2.loc.gov/ammem/wpaintro/wpahome.html

PICTURE CREDITS

TIMELINE OF THE DEPRESSION

1929
Hoover creates Farm Board
Stock-market crash (October)

1930
California begins voluntary repatriation
of Mexicans and Mexican Americans
Smoot-Hawley Tariff Act
Little Caesar, first great gangster movie
of the sound era
Ford cuts workforce by 70 percent
(June)
Drought strikes Midwest (September)

1931
Credit Anstalt, Austrian bank, collapses
(May 1)
All German banks close (July 13)
Britain abandons gold standard
(September 21)

1932
Norris-La Guardia Act
Congress approves Reconstruction
Finance Corporation (January 22)
FDR makes "forgotten man" radio
broadcast (April 7)
Repression of Bonus Expeditionary
Force by Douglas MacArthur (June
17)
Farmers' Holiday Association organizes
a farmers' strike (August)
FDR wins a landslide victory in
presidential election (November 8)

1933
Fiorello La Guardia elected mayor of
New York City.
Nazi leader Adolf Hitler becomes
chancellor of Germany
Assassination attempt on FDR by
Giuseppe Zangara (February 15)
FDR takes oath as 32nd president of
the United States (March 4)
National bank holiday (March 6)
Start of the Hundred Days: Emergency
Banking Relief Act (March 9)
FDR delivers first "fireside chat"
(March 12)
Economy Act (March 20)
Beer-Wine Revenue Act (March 22)
Civilian Conservation Corps
Reforestation Relief Act (March 31)
Emergency Farm Mortgage Act (May)
Federal Emergency Relief Act (FERA)
and Agricultural Adjustment Admin-
istration (AAA) created (May 12)
Tennessee Valley Authority (May 18)
Federal Securities Act (May 27)
London Economic Conference (June)
Home Owners Refinancing Act (June
13)
Banking Act; Farm Credit Act; Emer-
gency Railroad Transportation Act;
National Industrial Recovery Act;

Glass Steagall Banking Act (June 16)
73rd Congress adjourns (June 16)
FDR creates Civil Works Administration
(November)

1934
U.S. joins International Labour
Organization
Huey Long launches Share-Our-Wealth
Society (January)
Farm Mortgage Refinancing Act
(January 31)
Securities Exchange Act (June 6)
National Housing Act (June 28)

1935
Emergency Relief Appropriation Act
(April 8)
Soil Conservation Act (April 27)
Resettlement Administration created
(May 1)
Rural Electrification Administration
created (May 11)
Sureme Court rules NIRA
unconstitutional (May 27)
Works Progress Administration formed
(May 6)
Federal Music Project introduced (July)
National Labor Relations (Wagner) Act
(July 5)
Social Security Act (August 14)
Banking Act (August 23)
Public Utility Holding Company Act
(August 28)
Farm Mortgage Moratorium Act
(August 29)
Revenue Act of 1935 (August 30)
Wealth Tax Act (August 31)
Huey Long dies after assassination
(September 10)

1936
FDR wins 1936 election (November 3)
Gone with the Wind published
Charlie Chaplin's *Modern Times* is last
great silent movie
Supreme Court rules AAA
unconstitutional (January 6)
Soil Conservation and Domestic
Allotment Act (1936) (February 29)
Voodoo Macbeth opens in New York
(April 14)

1937
Wagner-Steagall National Housing Act
(September 1)
Supreme Court axes NLRB
CIO wins a six-week sit-down strike at
General Motors plant in Flint,
Michigan.
Supreme Court Retirement Act
(March 1)
Bituminous Coal Act (April 26)
Neutrality Act of 1937 (May 1)
Farm Tenant Act (July 22)

Revenue Act of 1937 (August 26)
National Housing Act (September 1)
Start of sit-down strike at General
Motors Fisher Body Plant in Flint,
Michigan, which lasts 44 days
(December)

1938
Amended Federal Housing Act
(February 4)
Agricultural Adjustment Act (1938)
(February 16)
Naval Expansion Act of 1938 (May 17)
Revenue Act of 1938 (May 28)
Food, Drink, and Cosmetic Act (June
24)
Fair Labor Standards Act (June 25)
Orson Welles' *The War of the Worlds*
broadcast (October 30)

1939
John Steinbeck's *The Grapes of Wrath*
published
Public Works Administration
discontinued
Federal Loan Agency created
Supreme Court declares the sit-down
strike illegal (February 27)
Administrative Reorganization Act of
1939 (April 3)
Hatch Act (August 2)
Outbreak of World War II in Europe
(September 3)
Neutrality Act of 1939 (November 4)

1940
In California the Relief Appropriation
Act is passed, raising the period of
eligibility for relief from one to three
years
Richard Wright's *Native Son* establishes
him as the era's leading black author

1941
American Guide series published for
the last time
Publication of James Agee and Walker
Evans' *Let Us Now Praise Famous Men*
Japanese bomb Pearl Harbor, Hawaii,
bringing U.S. into World War II
(December 7)

1943
Government eliminates all WPA
agencies

1944
Farm Security Administration closed

1945
FDR dies
Japanese surrender

INDEX